Stories and Legends Along the Maine Coast

By
William O. Thomson

To Chris & Connie & Becca
Best Wishes
Enjoy the book
Bill Thomson
11/4/08

Edited by
William M. Thomson

©Copyright 2007
ISBN-13: 978-0-9794854-0-4

Distributed by
'Scapes Me
135 Alewive Road
Kennebunk, ME 04043

Many Special Thanks To:

Jeremy Willey and Jodi Saucier
Owls Head, Maine

Henry Tilton
Kennebunk, Maine

Margaret Dixon
York Harbor, Maine

Virginia Spiller
Old York Hisorical Society
Librarian and Archivist

Paul M. Lawton, Esquire
Brockton , MA
Naval Historian

Hadley A. Schmoyer
Portland Harbor Museum
Curator

Jeanne P. Gross
The Museum At Portland Head Light
Director

*A very special thanks to
Bill Thomson, my son,
who edited the book*

Introduction

Maine's rugged coastline of bays, coves, harbors and peninsulas is well over two thousand miles long. Its many small towns are made up of beautiful ship captains' homes, saltwater farms, and weather-beaten sheds covered by lobster buoys and surrounded by lobster traps. The people who live in these homes have a distinct Maine accent and a philosophy of life that has been shaped for generations by the sea. From the stately to the homespun, their lives have been filled with intrigue and inspiration.

History is nothing more, and certainly nothing less, than the story of people going about their daily lives. It is the story of how people interact with each other and with their environment. Some of these stories are extraordinary, others mundane; many have become legends and a part of our folklore as they have been told, retold, and embellished over time. These stories reflect a time gone by that may seem simpler when compared to the complexities of our modern age, and yet they also reflect a period that may appear more challenging and difficult without our modern conveniences and technology. As we reflect upon the stories from our past, remember that the stories of our lives will become the history of the future.

Table of Contents

Strange Events
Along the Old Post Road

Captured By Hysteria – The Reverend George Burroughs

Route 1, called the Old Post Road and referred to as the King's Highway, passes through many of our coastal towns and some incredible events have happened along this road. One such event occurred in 1692 in Wells, Maine. The local minister at the time was George Burroughs and he became a victim of the bazaar hysteria that had taken over the people in Salem Village, Massachusetts. In just eleven months, ten young girls were responsible for causing the deaths of twenty good citizens and having over three hundred others held in jails and barns awaiting trials. Well, what was the crime committed by George Burroughs? He was in the wrong place at the wrong time.

Four years before preaching in Wells, Reverend Burroughs had been the minister in the Salem Village church. He had lived in the parsonage with his wife and two young daughters. The people liked him, but found him very outspoken. Thomas Putnam, a deacon and large contributor to the church, did not take too kindly to George. When the Reverend's wife died unexpectedly, Burroughs' meager salary did not provide him with enough money to bury her properly, and the minister had to borrow money from Mr. Putnam to purchase a casket.

After several months of mourning, Burroughs still missed his wife desperately. He decided to move up to Maine and preach here to try and build a new life for himself and his two young daughters. Before he left however, he neglected to repay his small debt or loan to Thomas Putnam. The case ended up in court and the judge ruled in favor of the minister. The church hadn't paid Burroughs a living wage, and because Putnam was the chief contributor to the church, the loan was cancelled. Three years later, four constables showed up at Burroughs' door in Wells,

5

arrested him, and took him back to Salem to face charges for the crime of practicing witchcraft.

Why would a thing like this happen? Well, in 1692 those ten young girls in Salem were pointing their fingers at many innocent people, accusing them of having familiarity with the devil, and the innocent victims were jailed for trial. Before the hysterias the girls used to meet secretly with a Barbados woman, Tituba, the Christian servant of the new village minister, Reverend Parris. Tituba talked about dancing, voodoo and black magic and she read the girls' palms. This was contrary to the Puritan values they had been raised with, and the girls knew that they were sinning.

Soon the youngest girl, nine year old Betty Parris, became sick. Whether this was from guilt or fear, others quickly followed; eleven year old cousin Abigail Williams; then Ann Putnam, the twelve year old daughter of Thomas and a real mischief maker. The girls performed some strange antics, like falling down, biting their lips to draw blood, and creating fits and convulsions.

Painting by William O. Thomson

The townspeople were alarmed and they wanted to know who or what was causing this to happen. The young girls would call out the name of some poor soul and that person would be locked up in jail. It was more than coincidence that most of the folks named were not liked by the girls' families or were not in the good standing of the town. Hatred, jealousy, family squabbles and land disputes all played a part in who was causing the girls' misery and tormenting their souls. The trials would become a circus as more and more names were called out from the witness box. The innocent victims didn't have a chance, and it seemed the girls were being prompted to settle old scores.

After Reverend George Burroughs was named by Ann Putnam and the others as one of their tormentors, a warrant was signed on April 30, 1692 for his immediate arrest. Marshall John Partridge of the Province of New Hampshire and Maine was assigned the task of delivering the minister to Salem for "examination for suspicion of confederacy with the devil."

When Partridge and three of his men arrived in Wells they explained the serious charges to George and told him of the chaos that was erupting in Salem. Being a kind religious man, Reverend Burroughs agreed to travel back to Salem with them. He believed he could help calm the hysteria and restore reality to the village through prayer, common sense and rational thinking. But Salem was beyond rational thought and Burroughs would later regret his decision.

Word of the Salem tragedy had reached the coastal villages of Maine and the residents knew that anyone who was accused would surely die. As the constables made their way south on The King's Highway, the militia of York had gathered along the road to mount an attempt to free the minister. They set up a roadblock on the dusty narrow road and waited. But before the party of five horsemen came to the bend in the road that separated York from Wells, Partridge and his men turned off and went around the little village. Apparently they had been informed of the attempt to free Burroughs. Today this road is called Witchtrot Road.

The constables reached the Piscataqua River and were ferried over to Portsmouth where they continued the journey. Just outside of Portsmouth they set up camp for the night and then a strange thing happened: a tremendous thunderstorm struck the campsite with vengeance. Cracks of thunder shook the ground and lightning ignited the soil. Trees were uprooted; wind gusted in a gale force; shadows leaped out from the trees as white currents of electricity flashed and bounced off the earth. Was this an attempt by the devil to help the Reverend escape? Perhaps George Burroughs was really a witch and he was practicing some dark art of sorcery. He could be evil; he could be wicked and sinister; he could have called the devil to his aid. There had to be a meaning for this threatening change of weather.

The once bold guards started to panic. They raced for cover and timidly buried themselves under some logs and stones. Burroughs wasn't shackled and he could have escaped, but because he believed that he was needed in Salem Village to help clean up the mess, he gathered up the horses and restored calm. Reverend Burroughs was a man of moral goodness. He knew righteousness; he had honor, principles and the strength of his convictions. He did what was right and for that he would die.

The next morning the group left for Salem. On May 4, 1692 John Partridge turned George Burroughs over to the judge and the Reverend was immediately placed in chains and held in a cramped jail with about thirty other people - many his former friends. The conditions were almost unbearable.

On May 9, Burroughs was interviewed in private by judges Jonathan Corwin, John Hathorne, Samuel Sewall and William Stoughton. They determined that Burroughs could not remember the last time he received communion; that his youngest child was not baptized; that although he owned toads, his Maine house was not haunted. Later that day he was brought into the room where the girls were testifying and the girls immediately started to quiver and shake. The judges noted that Burroughs seemed to be tormenting the young women.

Ann Putnam told the court how Burroughs had affected her. She saw him in her dreams and she was told that he had murdered his wife. "He beats me. He pinches me. He chokes me," she cried.

Other girls followed. One girl said his apparition had appeared and touched her on the arm and talked about the devil and sin. When the girls fell to the floor, kicked their feet and drew blood to their lips, things became chaotic. Later in the trial, a witness from Maine testified that Burroughs had demonstrated incredible strength by first lifting up a keg of molasses and carrying it by himself, then putting his finger in the barrel of a musket and holding up the weight of the long gun with just that finger.

Thomas Putnam, standing in the rear of the meetinghouse, must have grinned as he thought about the unpaid loan that the judge had legally ruled in Reverend Burroughs favor. The insecure Reverend Parris must also have been pleased. He had fanned the fires by preaching sermons that the devil was among the people and he suggested it could be a neighbor. Neighbors turned against neighbors and the town was in chaos and Parris became more powerful when people turned to the church.

George Burroughs was taken to the gallows to be hanged on August 19, 1692. Just before he died, Burroughs said the Lord's Prayer. He did not falter and every word was pronounced with clarity. Some of the Puritan spectators cried out that the minister was innocent because a devil couldn't say a prayer without stumbling. At that moment one of the constables blew smoke from his pipe into Burroughs' face and Burroughs coughed. "There is your proof," the guard scowled. "He coughed!" The noose tightened, and Burroughs life was over. His body was thrown into a gravel pit because witches were not allowed to be buried in Christian cemeteries for fear that their spirits would affect others. He was one of twenty people executed – nineteen from the hanging tree and one old man, Giles Corey, eighty-one years old, who was pressed to death under heavy granite rocks because the judges were trying to force a confession from him.

In October of that year, some semblance of sanity came back to the town. The last hangings took place on September 22, 1692 two days after Giles Cory was pressed to death. People finally realized the extent of the delusion that had occurred, and the epidemic of madness came to an end. In November the governor issued a pardon to all of the accused, who by that time included his own wife. The incidents of hatred between neighbors, revenge, jealousy and fear were over.

Attacked From the Woods - The Massacre of York

Back along the Old King's Highway we return to York, Maine, a town with a rich history. As the Salem witch fiasco was just getting underway, on January 25, 1692, members of the Abenaki Indian tribe came out of the woods and gathered near Chase's Pond, just outside of York Village. Near a rock that is still marked today, the war party removed their snowshoes and made final plans to attack the village. In the early morning hours of that cold day they swept from home to home, terrorizing and killing the residents. A good part of the town was ransacked, looted and burned. The men were brutally slaughtered in front of their wives and children. Over forty York men were killed and many of the women and children were kidnapped and marched off to Canada. The three hundred families in the community would have their lives disrupted forever by this dreadful event.

Snowshoe Rock
This rock, commemorated with a plaque, marks the area from which the Abenaki Indians launched their attack on the village of York.

The Reverend Shubael Dummer tried to negotiate with the warriors but two of the braves tore off his clerical gown and began to mock him. They made obscene gestures, humiliating the minister, while his neighbors stood by helplessly. Among the crowd of frightened citizens was four year old Jeremiah Moulton, who had just witnessed the scalping of his mother and father. He had seen enough, and attacked the Indians with his little fists. They were amused by his antics and had great respect for the little boy's courage. While the attention was focused on the child, Reverend Dummer found an idle horse, mounted it, and galloped away. A couple of Abenaki's chased the minister and fired a few shots, killing Dummer. During the melee, little Jeremiah Moulton was spared by escaping into the snowy woods where he was later found by another villager.

The Indians forced the captured women and children to follow them along a secretly marked trail to Canada. Supplies were hidden at certain destination points where the group set up shelter for the night. During the forced march, young children who couldn't keep up with their mothers were killed. Infants that couldn't stop crying were murdered so the war party could continue along the trail in silence. The sad state of affairs for the surviving prisoners didn't end in Canada, where upon their arrival many were sold into slavery or ransomed back to their relatives.

The day after the massacre a colonial militia group from Portsmouth marched over to York to bury the dead in a common grave. One reprisal for this massacre occurred thirty-two years later when the little scrappy Moulton boy, now thirty-six years old, exacted his revenge for the brutal slaughter of his parents. Jeremiah was a Captain in a guerilla force known as the Rangers and he had become one of the area's deadliest Indian fighters. One of their missions was to destroy an Indian encampment on the Kennebec River. This was a savage assault with the Rangers taking no male prisoners. Twenty-seven people were killed, including a French priest, a possible payback for the death of Reverend Dummer. Moulton continued hunting the tribes, took no mercy on the braves, and became a feared and formidable force protecting the frontiers in southern Maine.

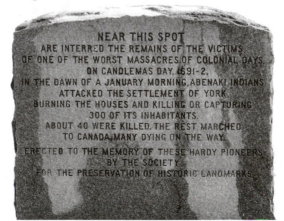

NEAR THIS SPOT
ARE INTERRED THE REMAINS OF THE VICTIMS
OF ONE OF THE WORST MASSACRES OF COLONIAL DAYS
ON CANDLEMAS DAY 1691-2,
IN THE DAWN OF A JANUARY MORNING, ABENAKI INDIANS
ATTACKED THE SETTLEMENT OF YORK,
BURNING THE HOUSES AND KILLING OR CAPTURING
300 OF ITS INHABITANTS.
ABOUT 40 WERE KILLED, THE REST MARCHED
TO CANADA, MANY DYING ON THE WAY.
ERECTED TO THE MEMORY OF THESE HARDY PIONEERS
BY THE SOCIETY
FOR THE PRESERVATION OF HISTORIC LANDMARKS.

Patience in the Old Gaol

The oldest jail in America, the Old Gaol, sits on top of a small hill in the center of the little village of York. Its thick stone walls enclose small dungeon-like cells. It has been reported that the cries of ancient prisoners have been heard from these old walls. Witches, thieves, drunks and gossips have all been held prisoner in its cells.

The story of Patience Boston is perhaps one of the saddest stories ever to emerge from the prison. Patience was born on December 26, 1711 in the Cape Cod area of Massachusetts. Her mother was Sarah Jethro, a full blooded Native American who was very active in the affairs of her Nosset tribe. Because of her mother's status, Patience was considered to be an Indian princess. Her mother died when she was only three, and Patience was given to a family who raised her as an indentured servant. For the rest of her short troubled life she rebelled against the Puritanical morals of her masters.

When she was nineteen, after many years of drinking and carousing, she asked to be sold to someone in Maine. Eventually Patience became a servant to the Trot family of Falmouth. By that time, she had already had two children, both of whom had died a short time after their births. While at the Trot's, she gave birth to another child whose father was also a Native American. Soon after, a terrible tragedy occurred when eight year old Benjamin Trot drowned in a well on the property. At the time of the accident only she and the boy were home, and when confronted with the boy's body, Patience reportedly confessed to murdering the child.

She was sent to the Old Gaol in York to await trial. Day after day went by as she and her infant were held in a dark dingy cell. Some say that she chiseled small lines in the granite of her cell to mark the time of her imprisonment. "Father" Moody, the parish minister, spent many hours with her to convince her of the evil of her ways. According to his account, she repented, was converted to God, and confessed her sins to him. After months of confinement she pleaded guilty at her trial.

Within a few days, on July 24, 1735, she was taken from her cell and marched through town to the gallows. She had been assured that her child would be placed in the care of a good family in York. In Reverend Moody's account, she repented her sins from the scaffold and asked God to have mercy on her child, on the executioner, and on the one hundred or so people who had gathered to witness her execution. As the rope was slipped around her neck she cried out her final words: "Lord Jesus, receive my spirit." She was buried in the paupers grave.

Legend differs somewhat from Father Moody's account of the execution. As Patience stood on the scaffold, her infant in her arms, she cried out to the crowd, pleading for someone to take

The Old Gaol
Built in 1653, this old jail housed all of the prisoners in the Maine territory during its early years. Patience Boston was held in one of its cells, pictured at left.

Photos courtesy of
Old York Historical Society

14

her precious child and give it a loving home. Just before the hangman tightened the noose, a young woman stepped forward and took the baby from her arms.

In any event, the child was sent to be raised by Jeremiah Moulton and his family, the same Jeremiah who had witnessed the savage scalping of his parents forty-three years earlier. Unfortunately the infant died two years later, but Patience was spared the torment of losing another child. It was probably a blessing that Patience died thinking that her baby would be secure.

Perhaps Patience Boston was innocent and the Trot boy accidentally fell into the well. She may have been the victim of an intolerant group of Puritans who coerced her into confessing as a warning to potential sinners. The history of many of our Puritan towns is full of stories of damnation for those who didn't conform to their strict moral code. Maybe the circumstances of her own difficult life caught up with her, and in a moment of irrational thought she really did push the boy into the well. Or, she may indeed have committed the horrible act of deliberate murder to revenge her harsh master, Mr. Trot. We will never know for sure.

A Veiled Sermon - Samuel "Father" Moody and
*   Joseph "Handkerchief" Moody*

Just across the street from the Old Gaol sits the First Parish Church of York. Many famous preachers have delivered sermons at the site of this church, none more renowned than Samuel Moody and his son Joseph.

In 1698, Samuel Moody, twenty-three years old and a chaplain at the time, was sent to York by Massachusetts authorities to preach to the settlers in this "frontier" town. Since the death of Reverend Dummer in the massacre six years earlier, the town had not had a permanent minister and it was feared that people might leave the small village. The York settlement had become a

15

strategic barrier to stop Native Americans from raiding coastal New Hampshire and Massachusetts towns.

Moody took quickly to his new community and within two years he was permanently ordained. Over the years, his parishioners were devoted to him and soon referred to him as "Father Moody," a term of great respect. As his reputation grew

The First Parish Church of York

throughout New England he was asked to speak at many other churches and he traveled extensively. He became friends with the great preachers of the day, including the English evangelist George Whitefield who visited Moody in York in 1744 and gave the sermon in the original First Parish Church.

Rev. Jotham Sewall, whose parents were members of Moody's congregation and relatives of his wife, gave an account of a time when Moody was asked to speak at a fellow minister's church. The preacher told Moody to expect people to leave the service early because that was their custom. Moody began his sermon by telling the folks that he would be addressing two types of people: sinners and non-sinners. He spoke for quite a while and then paused, continuing with the announcement that he was finished with that portion of his sermon addressed to the sinners. All the sinners were free to leave. As expected, no one moved and he continued preaching his lengthy sermon to a full church.

At the age of seventy, two years before he died, Samuel Moody accepted the position of chaplain for the troops who accompanied William Pepperell on a successful mission to capture Fort Louisburg on Cape Breton in Nova Scotia. Father Moody believed that God would intercede on behalf of the men and that the Catholic French would be driven from the fort. When he was asked to bless the food at a victory celebration dinner, the men feared their meals would be cold before the long-winded minister would finish. As Rev. Sewall relays the story, Moody simply lifted his hands and said, "O Lord, we have so much to bless thee for, we must refer it to eternity, -for time is too short: so bless our food and fellowship for Christ's sake." This was probably the only short prayer he ever delivered!

Samuel Moody ruled with an iron hand and he was a firm disciplinarian to his son Joseph, who was born in 1700. Like his father, Joseph had been educated at Harvard with a degree in Divinity, but when he returned to York he was more interested in teaching and working on town affairs than preaching. He seemed to be doing a good job as a schoolmaster in his early twenties, taking his students out of the classroom for practical learning experiences, fishing, and flying kites. He also became a record keeper for both the town and the county, and was appointed to the court.

His father however had his own ideas of how Joseph should conduct his life. When Joseph found a woman he deeply loved and wanted to marry, his father would not allow it. Samuel Moody also insisted that his son take up the ministry, and when he was traveling to other churches, he often required his son to preach for him in his absence. In 1730 Father Moody saw to it that a second parish was established in the Scotland area of York, and he persuaded Joseph to become the pastor.

Joseph finally married a woman who met his father's approval and their marriage produced four children. Like his father, he preached fine sermons and he was well liked by his parishioners. He still preferred his town record work and his parish school teaching to preaching however. The small size of the new parish just barely provided an income and when his wife died, leaving him the additional burden of caring for his children, the pressures of his life were too much of a burden for him to bear. He was deeply depressed and started to behave strangely.

One day he appeared in the pulpit with a handkerchief covering his face. When asked about it he provided no answers. He continued to wear the veil and would not make eye contact with his worshippers. He began to remain in the parsonage, spending all of his time alone, even barring the door to keep visitors from entering. He sent his children to live with others.

The church members began to resent his actions. When standing in front of the congregation he faced his back to them as he read his sermons, lifting the veil just over his lips so his words would carry. When he read scriptures from the bible he lowered the veil before he turned to face the congregation. No one would ever see his face again. Weddings, funerals, prayer services and general meetings became an embarrassment for all who had to deal with him. When he spoke, the veil seemed to dance with his voice in a strange up and down motion. He started to walk in the graveyard at night and would run away if he encountered another person. He ate his meals facing the wall. Finally the parishioners had enough of his strange behavior and they asked him to leave. Handkerchief Moody left the ministry and moved in to Deacon Bragdon's home.

The Scotland Area of York
Joseph "Handkerchief" Moody is buried in this cemetary. Shortly after donning his veil, he moved into the house visible in the background.

In 1745, when his father was on the Cape Breton expedition with Pepperell, Reverend Joseph Moody was somewhat recovered from his depression. He was asked to preach at a special service in the First Parish Church to send prayers for the success of the soldiers taking Fort Louisburg. Once again, Rev. Jotham Sewall's account of the service describes the scene as Moody, with his face covered by his veil, started to pray and plea to God that the fort would fall. Then suddenly he changed his tone and thanked God that the fort was taken and praised Him for His mercy. He closed with this: "Lord, we are no better than those that possessed the land before us; and it would be righteous if the land should spew out its inhabitants a second time." When Joseph Moody spoke those words, it was later determined that this was the exact time that the troops had taken the fort. Two years later, when peace was declared between France and England, the French returned to Fort Louisburg, thus "the land spewed out its inhabitants a second time."

Just before Samuel "Father" Moody died in 1747, the cornerstone was laid for a larger church in York Village, which is the building that remains today. Joseph "Handkerchief" Moody preached in the new church and was welcomed by his parishioners but he never removed the veil. People have speculated for years about his motives for hiding his face and many legends have been told. Nathaniel Hawthorne, a frequent visitor to York, wrote a short story entitled *"The Minister's Black Veil"* which popularized the tale. Was it a guilty conscience? Had the minister committed a sin? One often told narrative has the minister on his deathbed confessing to a friend that in his youth he had accidentally killed a friend in a hunting accident and had never admitted responsibility – the guilt had shamed him to hide his face. Joseph Moody died in 1753 with the veil still in place and the mystery unsolved.

Shipbuilding in Kittery, Maine

The Loyal Colonial Hero - Sir William Pepperell

Kittery, Maine is separated from Portsmouth, New Hampshire by the Piscataqua River. Piscataqua is a Native American term loosely meaning "the branch of two or three swift rivers." Many rivers flow into the Great Bay area of New Hampshire and combine in the Piscataqua to create one of the fastest flowing rivers on the American continent, with recorded speeds of over nine miles per hour. The flow of the river has created a fine deep water anchorage which rarely freezes over, and almost always has a constant breeze. This was a tremendous asset for the old wooden sailing ships that plied their trade in the busy harbor. Several small islands provided a protected and secure shelter from the open sea. Tall pines and hardwoods grew in the surrounding forest, so wood for masts and shipbuilding was plentiful.

Kittery would become one of Maine's leading seaport towns and its shipbuilding industry would become world renowned. From the days of John Paul Jones (the Naval hero of the American Revolution) whose ship the *Ranger* was built here, to the modern nuclear attack submarines that are serviced here today, Kittery takes great pride in the dynamic shipbuilding industry which still thrives under the banner of the Portsmouth Naval Shipyard.

Despite its name, this major shipyard is located on Seavey Island in Kittery, Maine. The yard was established in 1800, which makes it the oldest government run shipyard in America today. It is called Portsmouth Naval Shipyard because in the early days

Old York Historical Society Collection ,Gift of John Bardwell

Shipyard Circa 1925

Kittery didn't have a post office. All of the mail was sent to Portsmouth and then delivered by boat to the yard in Kittery.

The town of Kittery, officially incorporated in 1647, is Maine's oldest town and its major industry has always been shipbuilding. The original settlers were major contributors to this vital industry as carpenters, laborers, riggers, sail makers and fishermen. Many of their descendants still carry on these trades today.

Old York Historical Society Collection ,Gift of John Bardwell

Shipbuilders at the Portsmouth Naval Shipyard in Kittery, Maine

Every town has citizens that leave a lasting impact on the town's history. Kittery's famous citizen, Sir William Pepperell was a very influential man. Pepperell was the son of William Pepperell Sr. a prosperous Kittery merchant who made a fortune in the shipping industry. His wealth and influence were known all over the world.

Having grown up during the French and Indian War period, William Jr. had heard many stories of French war ships capturing and harassing his father's fleet and he came to despise the French.

The French were operating out of the heavily fortified Fort Louisburg on Cape Breton Island in Canada. Most military men at the time believed that the fort could not be captured; it was built solid and was totally self sufficient. However, in 1745 British authorities gave William Jr. the command of a campaign to attack and seize the fort. Despite his limited military experience, Pepperell was enthusiastic about his mission.

On March 24, 1745, ninety ships carrying four thousand men sailed from Boston, Massachusetts toward Cape Breton. Capturing Fort Louisburg, the strongest fort in North America, would be a remarkable victory, especially since the Yankee soldiers amassed for the battle were totally undisciplined and poorly trained. They were some of the most unkempt soldiers in American history as most didn't shave, didn't bathe, didn't clean their sloppy ill-fitting uniforms and they walked around barefoot. The training drills were extremely casual and sluggish and many of the soldiers spent their time drifting into the woods to get drunk. But on June 17, six weeks after the siege began, William Pepperell was able to capture the fort. His victory was a big step torward ending the French and Indian Wars.

The Pepperell Family Home in Kittery

In recognition of this great victory, King George II and the English government bestowed the title of Baronet on Pepperell. He became Sir William Pepperell and was the first American born person ever honored with a title by the English crown. However this acclaim was short lived, because Pepperell's heirs made the decision to remain loyalists when the revolution started, and the family moved to England. Their property in Kittery was confiscated and American militia troops were later quartered there.

Ironically, the first fortification in Kittery, which started construction in 1689, was named for William Pepperell Sr. At the time of the American Revolution the patriots did not appreciate British loyalists, regardless of who they were or what they had accomplished, and Fort Pepperell was renamed Fort McClary for Major Andrew McClary who was killed at the Battle of Bunker Hill. In 1844 a six sided blockhouse was built on the site and just before the Civil War, Hannibal Hamlin, of Paris, Maine was a company cook at the fort. He later became Abraham Lincoln's Vice President. The fort was decommissioned in 1918, but for two hundred and twenty-nine years it served as a vital link in the defense of our famous shipyard.

Revolutionary Patriot - John Paul Jones

On June 18, 1777 John Paul Jones was given his orders to take command of the ship *Ranger* which was being constructed and outfitted in Kittery. She was a sloop-of-war carrying eighteen guns, all six pounders, which meant that they fired six pound cannon balls. After advertising in the local paper for able seamen, a crew of one hundred and fifty men was chosen for the ship.

Jones had only lived in America since 1773. He was born in Scotland as John Paul, and started sailing as an apprentice on an English ship when he was thirteen. During his early years as a seaman, he sailed on ships that often stopped in America. By the age of twenty-one he was given command of his own ship, but on a subsequent trip to Jamaica, one of his men was severely disciplined and later died. Shortly thereafter, John Paul moved to Virginia and added the Jones to his name, perhaps to escape his past. Although he liked life at sea, he also thought he might like the life of a gentleman. At the beginning of the Revolution he joined the fledgling American Continental Navy as an opportunity to live in both worlds – as a captain facing danger at sea and commanding unruly sailors, while enjoying the authority and prestige that accompanies the title of "captain" or "commander."

In December of 1775, John Paul Jones, twenty-eight years old and a citizen of Virginia for only two years, was made a First Lieutenant in the Continental Navy. After five months he was promoted to the rank of Captain and given command of the *Providence*, a privateer ship with a crew of approximately seventy-five men. He soon established a remarkable record capturing over sixteen vessels and successfully engaging several British ships in combat in his first two months of command.

At thirty years old, Jones was ordered to proceed to Portsmouth, New Hampshire to take command of the brand new square rigger the *Ranger* which was near completion on Badgers Island in Kittery. Jones, a powerful man standing only five and a half feet tall, adapted well to Portsmouth and Kittery society. He was always properly dressed and never without a sword in his belt. His word was law and no one dared question his authority, commands or daring ventures. He was accepted by all as one of their own, a true aristocrat.

It took almost five months for Jones to assemble his prize crew, rig the ship and get her ready to sail. The same day that Jones had been given his orders to take command of the *Ranger*, congress had designated the "Stars and Stripes" as our national flag. When the ship arrived in France after completing its maiden voyage, the *Ranger* and a proud American crew under John Paul Jones received the first official salute ever given to the new flag by a foreign power. On Feb 14, 1778 in Quiberon Bay, a French squadron, which included the flagship of French Admiral La Motte Piquet, fired their guns as a salute to the Americans. This was an historical moment for the United States Navy and a proud event in American naval history.

The John Paul Jones House

This is the home in which John Paul Jones lived in Portsmouth, New Hampshire as the ship *Ranger* was being built and outfitted in Kittery.

Many people don't realize that a lot of the decks, gun ports and bulwarks on American privateer ships were painted bright red so the young hands and new recruits would not get sick or faint at the sight of blood which would splash everywhere during combat. Sea battles were hard fought and very bloody. Crewmen used swords, knives, axes, pistols, iron hooks, clubs - anything that could be used to inflict damage on the enemy.

During a cannon attack the captain would maneuver the ship to face his opponent broadside. Blacksmiths were important crew members as they created a variety of projectiles that were fired at the enemy: grape shot; bar shots; chain shot; and hot shots. Grape shot was a cluster of iron pellets or scrap metal which when fired would spread out across the deck, raising havoc with the ship's rigging and enemy crew. Bar shots, resembling two weights fused together, tore wooden rails and deck structures to shreds. Chain shot, two cannon balls connected by a chain, knocked down bowsprits and yardarms, tore through canvas and even splintered masts. Hot shots were heated cannon balls fired toward powder kegs or aimed at the powder room to ignite the area and cause an explosion. Splinters and shrapnel flew everywhere causing brutal injuries to arms, legs and eyes.

If the ships came in close contact the crew would attempt to secure the vessels together with grappling hooks. They then boarded the enemy ship carrying boarding pikes, long bayonets mounted to wooden poles, and smaller hand held weapons used to fend off attackers. Cast iron hand grenades were ignited and thrown down on the opponent's decks. Trained riflemen in the crows nest tried to pick off select crewmembers and enemy officers. Stink pots, earthen jugs filled with vile concoctions like sodium nitrate, decayed fish and human excrement, were thrown onto the decks to weaken resistance. Some jugs had an oxtail, or wick, which would ignite a chemical and release volumes of nauseating noxious smoke.

In the heat of battle, fear of capture was greater than the fear of injury or death. The British considered the American sailors to be traitors of England and prisoners were dealt with harshly. Many were confined to the rotting rundown British prison ship *Jersey* in New York Harbor. The men were stripped of all possessions and crammed below decks with rags for clothes, no toilet facilities, no fresh air and no exercise. They were hardly fed and disease was rampant. The sick and dying were spread out among the corpses. Each day the dead were brought up to the top deck and the brutal guards would designate some prisoners to carry the bodies into a nearby marsh for burial. All the filth from twelve hundred prisoners was dumped over the side of the ship into the river. The stench was horrific. Water taken from this sewer pit was used to cook the rotted meat served for dinner. Death was better than capture and the men fought hard.

When the battle was over the few doctors and medical personnel on the ship tried to help the injured crew. Oftentimes the captain and a ranking officer would assist. A primitive medical book offered instructions for fixing broken bones or tending to severe wounds. Hopefully the description of the wound was in the book and the person tending the injury could read! Anesthesia was just a piece of leather to bite down upon. Hygiene was a formidable challenge - it almost didn't exist.

Captains like John Paul Jones faced many challenges during long voyages coping with a group of unhappy and unruly sailors. The men grew tired of the monotonous daily diet of salt meat, hard bread, rice, beans, and duff (boiled flour pudding) infested with cockroaches, rats and worms. There was no mail or contact from home. The ships could experience days of dead winds during which they made no progress, or pass through storms and heavy running seas when even the most experienced sailors would get seasick. The men slept in cramped quarters for short periods between watches. Scurvy was prevalent because it was difficult to maintain an adequate supply of fresh fruits and vegetables.

John Paul Jones was Captain of the *Bon Homme Richard* on September 23, 1779 when he engaged the brand new and heavily armed English *Serapis* under Captain Richard Pearson in a sea battle off the coast of England. After a short cannon fight, Jones lost the side of his ship and had suffered severe damage, but he was able to grapple the two ships together.

"Has your ship struck? Do you surrender?" Pearson called out to Jones.

"No. I have not yet begun to fight!" Jones quickly replied.

Four hours later, both ships were ablaze. Dead and wounded sailors were everywhere amidst the destruction. *Bon Homme Richard* was taking on water faster than the pumps could empty it. At last, Captain Pearson called from the *Serapis* for an end to the shooting. Jones had won the battle. Two days later the *Bon Homme Richard* sank and Jones sailed the captured *Serapis* back to France with his prisoners and wounded.

The men who served with John Paul Jones would never consider themselves heroes. They were like the men and women of today – Americans serving their country the way they know best. They are the true American patriots. Our colonial men and women were proud. Our country was in its infancy; we didn't have many ships, we didn't have money, but our people had strength and conviction. Their effort established the sovereignty of this great nation.

The World's Largest Blast - Henderson's Point

The largest blast the world had ever heard up to that time took place on Henderson's Point in Kittery on July 22, 1905 at 4:00 P.M. Three hundred feet of solid ledge jutted out into the Piscataqua River and large ships had to be literally pulled around it with small boats and lines. It was a hindrance for the naval ships going in and out of the Portsmouth Naval Shipyard so the Navy decided to take it out with one blast. Fifty tons (one hundred thousand pounds) of explosives were used to destroy the point. Hundreds of large sticks of dynamite, eighteen inches long and three inches wide, were put into tubes that were inserted into holes that had been drilled into the solid granite. The wiring was hooked up and ready to go; Miss Foster would pull the switch.

The Navy had warned the residents within a half-mile of the blast area to open their windows. They were told to watch for flying debris and that the earth might tremble and crack plaster in their homes. Also, a river watch was set up for a possible tsunami wave that could result from the blast and cause considerable flood damage.

Kodak was marketing the entire event by heavily advertising film and developing. It was estimated that eighteen thousand people came to view the blast from across the river. Trolleys came in from towns as far away as Massachusetts and Kennebunk, Maine.

The switch was pulled at 4:10 P.M. and solid granite rocks exploded into the air, some as high as one hundred and twenty-five feet. A large tidal wave did indeed rise up from the river, but it didn't cause any damage. No buildings or property were destroyed and no one was injured. After the blast, the long ledge was twenty feet underwater and a clear passage around Henderson's Point was achieved. The Navy had direct access to one of their dry docks and ships sailing into the river would no longer have to be tugged and pulled around the obstruction. It was a great engineering success.

The Blast At Henderson's Point These three pictures show different views of the tremendous explosion that removed the ledge at Henderson Point in Kittery. Also, note the complimentary pass to watch the blast from special viewing areas.

EXPLOSION

HENDERSON POINT

SATURDAY, JULY 22, 1905, 4 P. M.

ADMIT BEARER TO OBSERVATION GROUNDS, PIERCE'S ISLAND, MOSES' ISLAND, GOAT ISLAND OR OLIVER PASTURE IN NEWCASTLE (CONNECTED BY PONTOON BRIDGE, FOOT OF GATES ST.)

GEO. H. KEYES

COMPLIMENTARY

All Photos: Old York Historical Society Collection, Gift of John Bardwell

The End of a War - The Treaty of Portsmouth

Another great event occurred in Kittery on September 5, 1905. The famous "Treaty of Portsmouth" which ended the Russo-Japanese War was signed in building #86 at the Navy Yard. (Remember: the shipyard is in Kittery but Portsmouth seems to get the credit for all of the success at the Navy Yard.)

The Russo-Japanese war started on January 8, 1904 when the Japanese attacked the Russians. Japan wanted complete control of Korea and they were willing to accept Russian control of Manchuria, but during the pre-war negotiations, the two sides couldn't agree. The Japanese had almost annihilated the Russian Navy with their superiority in successful sea battles. The Russian army, though not winning any battles, had used superior troop strength and armaments to defend their positions on land and the Japanese suffered heavy casualties. The deadly conflict cost tens of thousands of lives on both sides and had drained the treasuries of both countries. The Japanese had exhausted their troops, and the Russians were experiencing a period of political turmoil in their government. When President "Teddy" Roosevelt stepped in, using American status as a Pacific power to mediate an end to the war, both sides quickly agreed to treaty negotiations.

Old York Historical Society Collection, Gift of John Bardwell

Dignitaries Arriving In Kittery

Negotiators arriving at the Navy Yard to participate in the Russo-Japanese War peace talks. Many of them stayed in Newcastle, New Hampshire and were transported across the Piscataqua River by boat.

The Japanese wanted the talks to be held in Asia and the Russians wanted to negotiate in Europe. Teddy prevailed and the talks were held in the Portsmouth Harbor area, using the Portsmouth Naval Shipyard as the negotiating spot. It took thirty days of negotiations to settle the differences, and during that time the Kittery-Portsmouth area was the center of the world's attention.

When the Russian and Japanese delegates arrived they sailed into the harbor in their own warships. The Russian gunboat came in from the Maine side on the northeast, and the Japanese warship came in from the southeast on the New Hampshire side of the harbor. An American destroyer sailed between the two ships. Because the two countries were still at war, tension was in the air, and the American destroyer had its guns pointed at both ships The Navy had insisted that the Japanese and Russian ships aimed their guns up to the heavens above.

The dignitaries, Jutaro Komura from Japan and Sergei Witte from Russia, and other important delegates were housed in the famous "Wentworth by the Sea" hotel. The hotel was built in 1874 in Newcastle, New Hampshire at the mouth of the Piscataqua River, next to the Maine border. The hotel had three hundred rooms, fresh water from deep artesian wells, beautiful gardens, a golf course, elegant dining, a small marina and an ice house which was a necessity in 1905. President Theodore Roosevelt also wanted a place with superior service, a neutral setting, an area of security (the Navy Yard) and a local population that would be enthusiastic about tourists and visitors. Since air conditioning was unavailable, the pleasant days, cool nights and sea breezes along the coast of New Hampshire and Maine were very attractive.

The large contingent of international reporters covering the treaty negotiations stayed all around the Portsmouth area. For their convenience, a transatlantic cable was installed which was linked to Rye, New Hampshire, the next town down the coast. The local people were in their glory – their wonderful area was being promoted around the world and the many reporters, visitors and dignitaries were spending a lot of money. The town's socialites hosted numerous parties, some very elegant affairs and others less highbrow. At one of the more jovial affairs two Japanese diplomats were highly embarrassed when they fell off a pier into the river and had to be rescued. Trips to museums, concerts and sporting events were planned, as well as boat cruises out to the Isle of Shoals. President Roosevelt never appeared at the conference, preferring instead to stay at his seasonal home in Oyster Bay, New York, but he kept in touch daily with his advisors.

After thirty days of intense discussions, a treaty, written in French, was finally hammered out and signed on September 5, 1905 at 3:47 P.M. The Japanese would still have interests in Korea; Russia would return Manchuria to China and give Japan the southern half of Sakhalin Island. No reparations were paid by either party. This was the first time that a non-European power had defeated a European country and it gave the Japanese power and confidence that many people feel led them to attack the United States at Pearl Harbor on December 7, 1941.

In any event, the Treaty of Portsmouth was signed in Kittery, Maine and thirty-six years of peace in the Pacific followed. Church bells rang from the steeples of the seacoast churches while guns fired salutes; fireworks exploded overhead and people

Building #86
Site of the Peace Talks

Reporters from all over the world covered the negotiations in Kittery and followed the participants closely.

Photos: Old York Historical Society Collection, Gift of John Bardwell

danced in the streets. President Theodore Roosevelt received the Nobel Peace Prize in 1906 for his efforts in ending the war. The far reaching consequences and impact on the world from this document drafted on the Maine side of the Piscataqua River just over one hundred years ago will not be forgotten.

A Ghostly Castle - Portsmouth Naval Prison

Just northwest of Henderson's Point, directly across the harbor from the "Wentworth by the Sea" stands an eerie abandoned building. It rises up from the middle of the river on Seavey Island with the profile of an old deserted castle. Its interior encompasses over two hundred and sixty thousand square feet and the view from its windows is unsurpassed. Most of the people who spent time here however rarely enjoyed the scenery, and the building has been vacant since 1977.

The castle is the Portsmouth Naval Prison, and along with many of the "real bad boys" from the Navy, it was the temporary housing for many of America's prisoners of war. In 1898 a small building located at the present site held over thirteen hundred Spanish-American War prisoners. In 1908 construction started on a new facility and by 1912 it would become the second largest prison in the world! Over its sixty-nine year history more than eighty-two thousand prisoners were incarcerated here.

The prison was not a hotel and its "guests" were not here for rest and relaxation. Prisoners were held in cells that measured only six feet by ten feet and were furnished with only two bunks and a toilet. The cells were stacked four stories high and they were built away from the windows, with a corridor running between the windows and the cells. The top floor of the structure was open. The prison contained a print shop, auto repair shop, kitchen, bakery, laundry, and carpenter shop.

The Marine guards who supervised the prisoners had a reputation for being tough; they were the authority and the prisoners knew it. Solitary confinement in the black hole; bread and water for three days; a good rap on the ankles by a guard established discipline and maintained order. Most of the inmates were hardcore criminals and the Marines kept them in line.

Throughout its history, only one successful prison break occurred at the prison. A few years after World War II, three men fled to the river, swam to a lobster boat, and made their way to Newcastle, the peaceful little town across the Piscataqua. The swim against the fast moving current almost killed the escapees. To the relief of the local townspeople, the three men were quickly captured and returned to the prison, where you can be assured they wished they had never attempted their escape.

At the present time, the Navy has no plans for the future of the building. The beautiful circular iron staircase with its mahogany rails is amazingly still in place, but the condition of the rest of the structure is deplorable. Bars in the cells are rotting; numbers over the cell doors are barely visible under the dirt, dust and cobwebs; rust, litter, broken windows and graffiti are everywhere. Pigeons, bats and mildew are in every dark corner of the immense, cold, damp space. It's the perfect climate in which to find a few ghosts roaming the empty halls.

Is the prison haunted? Ghostly lights have been seen moving between the windows. Elusive shadowy figures carrying lights that reflect in their colorless, corpselike faces have been seen in the cells. Who are these loathsome, ugly creatures? Engulfed by the revolting smell that permeates the rotted walls and drifts through the broken windows, a visitor might believe that a despicable character from the past is sending a message. Perhaps it's a request for a pardon of a misdeed or felony that occurred years ago. It could be an attempt to try and amend a past action or reprehensible crime. We will never know. As long as the Navy has no plans for the property, people will still sense these specters and phantomlike creatures behind the vacant prison's walls. Let them taunt, scoff and carry on, but greet them with a doubtful eye and don't allow them to hoodwink or bamboozle you. Old buildings with a mysterious past can free the imagination to run wild in a naïve mind. Good luck!

Myths and Legends Along the Coast

A Famous Visit by a Sea Serpent

On August 14, 1817 a sea serpent was spotted in Casco Bay. More than fifty different people wrote accounts of this sighting, and all of the descriptions matched, despite the fact that most of the people didn't know each other and had observed the strange creature from different points along the bay. The animal was between seventy and one hundred feet in length. It had eight separate hunches, or areas in its back about four feet apart that showed above water. As the creature swam, the wake it left could be followed for a half mile. The body was as big around as a mid-sized barrel. The scaly rough skin was a deep dark green and slick brown color. A head with piercing ruby red eyes sat upon its white neck and its three foot long tongue looked like a forked harpoon. Tiny sharp teeth ringed the monster's mouth.

Captain Titus Cutter was one of the ship captains who had a firsthand view. The ugly creature was about one thousand yards off his stern when it turned toward the boat and seemed to set a course directly for the small ship. The animal swam underwater and Titus guessed its speed to be about nine knots, or close to seven miles per hour. It surfaced about forty feet from the starboard side and then he noticed its gross tongue. Titus had his pistol loaded, but thought better of shooting at the animal as he didn't want to provoke it in any way. He recalled a sea story he once read about a sea serpent that wrapped its body around a ship, dove under the water and carried the ship and crew to the very depths of the Atlantic. This wasn't in Captain Cutter's plan. The creature sank down into the water like a large link of chain and surfaced on the port side of the boat before swimming off at the same pace. These were very anxious moments for the captain and his crew as they watched the creature move swiftly away with its head above water.

For the next month the creature was sighted several times, and like Captain Cutter, no one attempted to engage the monster in any way. Several sightings of the creature were also recorded in July of 1819. Most of the people who saw the serpent were reliable. Scientists who followed the events classified the creature as a prehistoric reptile (Plesiosaurus). A minister who saw the creature and was known for accuracy and truth gave the same account as the ship captains. Fishermen who had been to sea all their lives said they had never encountered anything like this. Reports of this strange creature were also recorded in at least six different years between 1820 and 1890.

As these stories are passed down for generations, many people doubt their authenticity. Some think the sightings were nothing more than a mass hallucination, or simply attention-getters. Some felt that the stories were concocted by the hotels along the shore, to get people to visit the seaside resorts, but in 1817 and 1819 there were no crowds trying to get to our shores. Many people feel that the existence of a sea serpent is an established fact. Fishermen never know what they will find in their nets. Somewhere in the depths of the Atlantic, in the dark caves and ridges, an unknown monster could hide and survive.

Visitors or Occupants? The Strange Presence of Ghosts

Living along the Maine coast presents many opportunities to experience the unknown. Northeast storms, dense fog and eerie winds can call forth strange whispers, shadows, silhouettes, reflections and sounds that suggest someone, or something, is lurking in the darkness. Is it possible to walk in the footsteps of some old spooky myth and share a weird earthly experience? Ninety-nine percent of all ghostly encounters can be explained, but what about that last one percent?

Many people have witnessed some dramatic events which happen often enough that they seem commonplace, though they remain unexplained. Room temperature suddenly drops; a cold spot forms in a part of a room, or on a warm surface like a handrail; an odor of perfume, flowers or tobacco fills a room. Sometimes when no one is present, voices or the sounds of footsteps running, walking or climbing stairs can be heard. Strange lights can be seen flashing, or a beam of light floats back and forth across a room. Most people don't experience these mysterious happenings, but we are fascinated by them. The folks who live with the unknown are as sane and sound as we are, so we have to put some stock into their chilling tales. Here are some friendly experiences that continue over and over.

One of our small towns boasts of a ghost that haunts four houses near the railroad station. No one knows the reason for its presence, but it has been very active for the last fifty years. The four houses are across the tracks from each other and they have all experienced strange happenings. Lights with pull chains are turned on; light bulbs are unscrewed from their sockets. At one house a chandelier fell from the ceiling and crashed through a coffee table. Not one piece of crystal glass was broken, although the coffee table was smashed and it wasn't even sitting directly under the chandelier! Items have been moved to different locations in the cellar. Tools are missing from the workbench and later found on a table across the basement, as though they had just been used and not put back in their proper place.

There is a strange story that is told about one of the four houses. When the railroad first came to town, Mr. and Mrs. Joseph Perkins built a house near the station. Joe was the ticket collector and conductor for the old B&M train. With his wife Sarah they had a lovely garden around the house, and they kept the property shiny right up to the time of their deaths, at the age of eighty-three, just six months apart. Because they did not have any children, they left the house to their nephew, Bob. Unfortunately, he was not a housekeeper or a proud home owner; he didn't paint,

Painting by William O. Thomson

39

repair, cut grass, or water the beautiful flowers that Sarah had spent many precious hours grooming and growing.

The third year Bob lived in the house the neighbors noticed a strange thing during the second week of August. The paint peeled off the house, and in what seemed like one day, the grass and garden around the house turned brown as though scorched. Bob was down on his luck, he had lost his job and was nearly penniless, so he sold the house the following January. Throughout the next year, the new owners put the house back into shape, planting a garden which produced vegetables that were the pride of the neighborhood. They were very particular and took great pride in the property. Since they restored the property to its pleasing condition, they have experienced a lot of good fortune and their lives are happy and joyful. The new owners and their neighbors all credit this turnaround to the ghostly presence of Joe and Sarah Perkins, who could not rest in peace until they knew their beloved home was cared for properly.

Unusual events have occurred over and over again at another house. The owners have a nice recreation room in the basement with a pool table and a dart board. When the family is finished playing a game of pool or darts, they put the darts and pool balls in a storage case and hang the pool sticks on a wall rack. At different times, in the middle of the night, the clank of pool balls or the thump of darts hitting the wall can be heard from the upstairs bedrooms. In the morning, the balls are all over the pool table, the sticks are on the floor, and the darts are stuck in the board. Perhaps sensing a strange presence, the family dog will not go down the cellar stairs.

One of the children in this house also is able to sense a presence. Over the last several years she claims that when she has been downstairs alone she has sensed a cold spot, and for a few seconds has felt someone staring at her. She has also heard coat hangers rattling in the closet when nobody was in the room with her. Her uncle Herb had lived with her parents in the home for five years before he died, and he enjoyed playing pool and darts. He had dark piercing eyes and her family said he owned several jackets which he hung in the basement closet.

Many strange things have happened in a wide variety of houses along the Maine coast. Pictures have been turned around on walls and bureaus. Wind-up toys started performing at strange times of the day or night, or two wind-up clocks stop at precisely the same time. Windows and doors open, close, or even lock by themselves. One house has a mantel that will not hold a certain candle holder. Every time it is left on the mantel it falls to the floor. Rocking chairs rock when no one is in a room. Radios and televisions are turned on and off, lights flicker, furniture is rearranged and toilets flush at will. The now forgotten sound of a typewriter clicking away has been heard, as have clock chimes, strange voices, pianos and organs, when there are none of these things in the home.

Perkins Cove in Ogunquit, Maine is a place where many ghosts seem to make their presence known. Captain Jeremiah from the area is buried along the side of an old road lined with stone walls, old farms and pretty trees. He died around 1870 and the old man doesn't want anyone tampering with his final resting place or grave marker. Jeremiah was a proud old man with a

Perkins Cove ~ Ogunquit, Maine

solid reputation as a good captain. During his many years at sea as captain of a ship he was used to being alone, and it is believed that he wants to keep to himself even in death. He has been seen hovering over his gravestone when anyone approaches too closely. The captain is dressed in his uniform, boots and all, and he has a full white beard. He appears for several seconds and then vanishes, but if someone persists in the area, he will appear again and stare directly at them. The town highway department is well aware of his final resting ground and they treat it with great respect, and many local joggers cross the road before they come to his stone.

Eva Gray, an opera singer who died October 31, 1904 while performing on stage at the Biddeford City Theater, seems to have made this small theater in Maine her final home. She was only thirty years old when she sang her last song titled *"Good Bye, Little Girl, Good Bye."* Her three year old daughter was in the front row. Eva's silver toned voice filled the auditorium as she sang the words of one of the most beautiful comforting songs ever written. When the last words resonated off the walls, she clutched her heart and fell to her knees. A thunderous applause followed as Eva was assisted off the stage. She died in her dressing room a short time later.

It appears Eva has never left the theater. Strange sounds have been heard in the dressing room: a knocking in the wall; footsteps trying to leave; an almost inaudible tiny voice. Some of the actors rehearsing and performing at the theater have heard a strange unexplained rattling sound and they have seen stage props moving around. Eva's actions demonstrate more of a loving nature than a scary one however, and the theater workers seem to like her being around. They experience a comforting sense of happiness in her presence.

In Port Clyde, Maine the old mansion home of Captain Leon Baxter has an intriguing story. He moved up from Kennebunkport in 1812 with his wife Elsa. Poor Elsa liked Kennebunkport and she could not adjust to the change. There were very few homes in Port Clyde, and she liked company and missed her old friends.

Captain Baxter could be at sea for a year or longer on a single journey, and while he was gone his wife worried about him. So much could go wrong on a voyage that she prayed constantly for his safe return. At least in Kennebunkport, a busier seaport, she might get word from another ship that had crossed paths with her husband in his travels. At Port Clyde she rarely received any news.

Captain Baxter sailed out of Port Clyde in August of 1813 with a load of clapboards. After stopping in Baltimore, the ship headed off to the Caribbean and planned a quick return trip home. The voyage should have been between three and four months. He promised his wife he would be home by Christmas. In 1813 the United States was at war with England and ships like Baxter's were very vulnerable. He carried three six pound cannons and the crew was armed with muskets, swords, knives, axes, and pistols. If cargo ships encountered enemies at sea they would be at a tremendous disadvantage, and if they were captured or sunk, communication was so bad that family members might never be informed.

Baxter and his crew were never heard from again, but Elsa never gave up. She waited alone, year after year, for her husband's ship to appear on the horizon and come into port. She prayed that he would return, but to no avail. She was very lonely with no family in the area and few friends to look after her. She died in the home several years later of a broken heart.

Since 1824, every owner of the Baxter House in Port Clyde has felt Elsa's presence, especially on the widow's walk and the upper floor. On days when the air is motionless people have felt a cool breeze push past them when they were out on the widow's walk. Elsa roams between the two bedrooms upstairs, looking out to sea. Guests and family members who have slept in these rooms have woken up in the middle of the night gasping for air, feeling stifled. Some people have felt a pressure being applied to their body, as though a pair of hands was pushing down on their shoulders. Bedcovers have been turned down in these rooms and some of the owners' pets never entered the rooms.

One of the oddest things that happened was when a twenty-one year old girl sleeping in the room heard what sounded like a lady softly crying. The noise seemed to come from the window. When she walked over to it she couldn't distinguish anything unusual, but her bare feet felt some water drops on the old soft pine floor. She always wondered if these were Elsa's tear drops as she stood by the window whispering, "I'm waiting for you. I'm waiting for you. Please return." It took about one hundred years of waiting for Elsa to finally move on. Since 1913, none of the homeowners have reported any unusual activity in the upstairs rooms. Hopefully, Elsa has found her peace. Perhaps the captain contacted her and she has joined him in their rightful place.

For years these Maine myths, legends and folklore have been repeated. One such story is about a man named John Newton who was about to be executed for a crime he swore he didn't commit. John was steadfast in claiming his innocence and just before he died he declared that no grass would grow on his grave for one hundred years. He was innocent and he was right. Despite many attempts, the cemetery caretakers couldn't get grass to grow. But after a hundred years, when the grass finally came out, it grew in the shape of a cross!

Pirates and Murder on the Isles of Shoals

Edward Teach, the notorious pirate also known as Blackbeard, lived on Appledore Island, a Maine island that is off the coast of Kittery and a part of the Isles of Shoals chain. He used Appledore as a temporary base for his pirate ventures in 1717, and supposedly he buried part of his treasure here. In 1812 Sam Haley was walking around the island when he discovered several silver bars worth about $3,000 buried under a flat rock that covered three feet of sand. Mr. Haley used the money to build the Smutty Nose Harbor Pier and a breakwater which still stands today. Treasure hunters keep looking, but no treasure has been found since.

Pirates had a reputation for being bold, reckless and lawless. They cruised from the Caribbean along the east coast to northern Maine, looking for ships to board and conquer, confiscating the cargo to claim as their own, and murdering or marooning the crews. Blackbeard was among the most feared of these pirates. Legend has it that he enhanced his reputation by twisting wicks laced with gunpowder in his hair, and lighting them on fire during an attack on an opposing ship.

Blackbeard abandoned his ninth wife on the Isles of Shoals. They had lived in a hovel which he had thrown together from driftwood and debris that washed up on Appledore. One morning he spotted a small British warship approaching the island and he told his wife to hide and he hollered, "Goodbye! I shall return." He sailed off in his ship and never returned. Mrs. Teach was left to fend for herself. She struggled to find food and keep warm, but soon succumbed to the elements. To this day she has been seen roaming around the island, still wearing the white dress she had on when Blackbeard sailed away. She floats through the air around Babb's Cove, named for Philip Babb, another pirate and brutal tavern keeper. Some people have heard her mumbling, "He shall return. He shall return."

Louis Wagner's ghost has been seen and heard roaming around Portsmouth and on Smutty Nose Island, another of the Isles of Shoals. He was accused of a very brutal robbery and murder that occurred on the island around midnight on March 5 and 6, 1873. He had rowed nine miles out to Smutty Nose from Portsmouth after hearing some Norwegian fishermen on the docks say that they had left their wives and their savings back home on the island. Wagner had lived on the island and he knew these families well. The three women, Maren, Anethe, and Karen, were staying in the same house. Louis approached the house quietly, then snuck in and hit Karen over the head with a chair. Maren and Anethe escaped to the yard, where he caught up with Anethe and murdered her with an axe. Maren escaped and hid in a small cave now called Maren's Rock. Louis returned to the house where he strangled Karen and then ransacked the place looking for the money. He found only fifteen dollars and retreated to his boat, leaving a bloody trail of footprints in the snow. He then rowed nine miles back to Portsmouth.

Early the next morning Maren came out from hiding and summoned help. She was able to identify Louis Wagner as the perpetrator of this horrendous crime. Louis in the meantime had boarded a train for Boston, but he was quickly apprehended by the Boston authorities and was returned to Portsmouth to stand trial. A mob of two thousand angry people met the train and wanted to lynch him on the spot.

The trial was held a short time later and the jury delivered their guilty verdict in just fifty-five minutes. Louis Wagner died on the gallows. His apparition has been seen many times around the harbor. By his frantic motions, he appears to be agitated. He is probably seething - troubled that a jury could find him guilty. A power boat today couldn't get out and back to Smutty Nose in

Old York Historical Society Collection, Gift of John Bardwell

An Early View of Portsmouth Harbor
This is the water side of Ceres and Bow Streets, where the ghost of the convicted murderer Louis Wagner has been seen roaming through the night.

the time that Louis was supposed to have rowed both ways. He also must have felt that Maren was so distraught by the tragedy that she was mistaken when she identified him, especially since this all happened around 1:00A.M. in the darkness of night. From all the speculative evidence presented at the trial against Louis, he might have the right to sulk and fret and show his anguish as an agitated apparition. Or perhaps his not being able to rest is further punishment for his crime.

Other Captains, Keepers, and Mysterious Events

The first ghostly experience ever recorded in Maine happened in Machiasport in 1799. The Blaisdel family had recently purchased a home from Captain George Butler and soon after they moved in, they heard strange noises from the basement. When they investigated the sounds they noticed a bright light in the cellar, and on one occasion it became the shape of a human figure. The ghost who haunted the house was Butler's deceased wife, whose maiden name was Nelly Hooper. She first appeared when she discovered that George Butler had remarried. You see, George had sworn on Nelly's deathbed that he would never marry again, and Nellie was there to harass him and his new wife. She hadn't figured that George would sell the old house to Abner Blaisdel and move over to his new wife's home. It took about five months for Nellie to figure out her husband was no longer living in the house, and after the town minister visited her she disappeared.

Another sea captain who haunts a local house in a back cove has made his presence known many times. One event, never to be forgotten, occurred on a Thanksgiving Day. The husband and wife were accustomed to the old timer's presence and they tried to humor him. While preparing the Thanksgiving dinner, the husband teased his wife about setting a place for the old captain. She set the table for just six: mom, dad, grampa, nana and the two children. "Let the old man go hungry," she sharply replied.

She left the dining room and returned to the kitchen. I guess the old sea captain didn't like her answer, for minutes later the entire table setting for six landed on the floor in a broken heap, as though someone had pulled the tablecloth out from under all the dishes. The old man's action was a bit vindictive, something out of character for this usually passive spirit. "I guess the old captain is upset with me," the woman remarked.

The age of a structure, its condition, the weather or climate, all create an atmosphere in which hauntings can occur. Many Maine lighthouses are perched on high granite ledges and are surrounded by wind, mist, fog, and the shrill lonely cries of seagulls. The flashing beacons, the crashing waves, changing tides and the smell of the salty sea can all cause the imagination to create many spooky stories. Most of the stories can be explained, but once again, what about those that can't? Are these lighthouses haunted? Here are a few hauntings that have been reported over and over again.

At Seguin Light Station a ghost of a woman plays a piano, but there is no piano in the lighthouse. Also a young girl has been seen bouncing a ball on the grounds. Brass has been polished overnight and tools have been taken and later returned. Voices and laughter have been heard throughout the house. The beds in the upstairs rooms have been shaken while people sleep.

On Ram Island Light in Boothbay Harbor, fires have been seen at night on the beach, but the next day when investigated, no ashes were found. Whistles have been heard blowing a warning to ships passing too close to the rocks, but there is no fog whistle on the island. An old ghostly figure of a man has been seen running back and forth across the island.

In several Maine lighthouses, passing ship captains have seen figures in the windows waving their ships away from the rocky ledges. Some captains have heard cries warning them to stay away. Lamps have been tended when no one has been there to tend them. Fog horns have been turned on or off on deserted islands. Jackets and hats have been thrown off hooks, and bureau drawers have been emptied. Furniture has been moved around

Seguin Light Station
This remote island lighthouse is known for its many reports of strange unexplainable events.

and windows opened and closed. Cries of a woman or child have been heard and cold spots swish by keepers as they climb the spiral iron stairs that go up into the towers.

Faces and apparitions have appeared out of nowhere; pipes are banged for no reason, sometimes in an apparent code. An unusual smell fills a corner or closet of a small room. Doors that have been locked and secured have been found open. Stove burners have been turned up or off when left unattended. Food has been thrown across a room. Dishes have rattled and paint and supplies have mysteriously disappeared. Both hot and cold breathing has been felt on necks and footsteps have been heard on catwalks. Voices have been heard, some humming or singing. Puffs of pipe smoke have suddenly appeared.

Some of these specters, or lighthouse ghosts, have been given names by the keepers who lived with them: "the old captain," "the lady in white," "Sally," "Kate," "old John," and "the little girl." Many of these ghostly figures were supposedly the victims of a traumatic death that occurred on the premises, such as a drowning accident. Others were tragic figures who died from a broken heart. Some may be the shadowy spirit of a dedicated keeper who refuses to leave because of an emotional attachment to the light, or a feeling that he is still needed. One thing for sure is that lighthouses captivate the minds of the viewers and set their imaginations free.

Ghostly apparitions have been seen and felt over and over again for hundreds of years. We do not know what they are or how they are formed, but there is evidence of their existence. Realtors have ghost clauses written into some real estate contracts for homes where unusual events have occurred because apparitions and strange things do appear and happen. These experiences are passed on to the next owners of the property, suggesting that a family ghost or spirit of the past is not yet willing to leave. Would you want to live in one of these houses? Like walking in a graveyard at midnight, or sleeping in an abandoned lighthouse tower, each of us must decide how far we want to test our beliefs as our nerves become frazzled, or even unraveled, as we explore the unknown.

Portland Breakwater Light

Original Painting by Bill Sachs

"Signal of Hope"

Maritime Adventures ~ Life Aboard Ships at Sea

Between 1865 and 1900, it is estimated that ten percent of the total American merchant ships sailing all over the world were captained by men from Searsport, Maine. Many of these ships had been built in this town and they were owned by its residents. This was an impressive achievement for a small Maine town.

Sailing a ship without engines, with nothing more than the wind and tall masts, hundreds of lines, each with a different name, and yards and yards of canvas to move the ship forward, was always an adventure. A good sailor had to know how to read the climate and sea. He knew how dangerous and mountainous the ocean waves could suddenly become and he knew how fast an angry sea could swallow a boat. Almost every cruise included some drama, comedy and suspense.

Old York Historical Society Collection, Gift of John Bardwell

Early Wooden Ship Construction

The captain was in total command of the ship and he made every decision. When navigation became difficult he might not leave the ship's wheel for hours at a time. During severe storms, some captains were known to tie themselves into a chair placed next to the wheel and they would only catnap when they got the chance. Captains were informed of every condition, at all times, because a bad decision or wrong calculation could result in death for all.

Many navigational terms, including references to a ship, use the female term of "she." "She is blowing up a storm." "She sails fast and smooth." The reason is that seamen and their ships are in a close partnership, with each needing the other to survive. They are completely dependent upon each other: the sailors perform their tasks and the ship responds, and when the ship takes some unexpected action the sailors must respond. The ship becomes the personal partner of the man, hence a wife, and the partners set a course and work together for survival.

The captain and crew maintained a steady vigil throughout the duration of a voyage. Their maps and instruments were not always accurate. Sometimes their only guides were the stars. They learned to recognize every moan, creak, and groan of a ship, to know what was normal and to identify what was not. They knew the wind force and direction, and they were aware of the ever changing patterns of the massive sea. The sky and ocean color; the flow of the current; the setting sun; the billowing clouds and gentle shifts in the weather were all part of the sailor's sense.

Sometimes a captain would take his wife and/or family on a voyage. One woman from Searsport sailed side-by-side with her husband many times over several years. On one such cruise as they were sailing around the Horn on the way to San Francisco, the captain was taken sick and she took command of the one thousand eight hundred ton ship. She had the first mate shackled in irons, and no confidence in the second mate. She knew how to navigate the vessel and she carried out the task as well as a full-fledged captain. The severity of the Cape Horn winds blew the sails out of the rope hooks. Hail and tides running in cross directions drove water onto and below decks. Visibility was zero. Her skin was caked with salt and her strength and vigor were sapped. She lashed herself to the wheel and had the crew lash themselves to their stations. Huge seas crashed across the deck, the wind tore the sails apart, the crew was frozen and the ship was running at a huge list and being driven toward ledges and floating glaciers. It took fourteen days of exhausting labor but she made it. The crew had nothing but praise for her when they finally sailed into the calm Pacific. The captain recovered and sailed the ship on the return trip home while his wife returned to their cabin to read and finish a bedspread and a lace pillow she had started. What a woman she must have been!

So many Searsport families made their living on the high seas that it was common to run into other families from back home when they were berthed in foreign ports. Here they visited each other while the ships were loaded and unloaded. They exchanged tidbits of news and swapped stories of their adventures. Sometimes one of the captains would ask his "neighbors" on board for a special party or celebration. While the captains conducted their ships' business, the children and wives would

Wooden Ship at Sea
Note laundry hanging between masts.

U.S.S. Enterprise
This 1375 ton steam and sail sloop of war was built in Kittery in 1877

Photos: Old York Historical Society Collection, Gift of John Bardwell

54

tour the port and get a firsthand education about the culture and lifestyle of another part of the world.

At the time of the Civil War, the great era of these beautiful sailing ships was ending as their numbers decreased. Steam driven ships had started to appear and the wooden square riggers had seen their heyday by the late 1800's. The nineteenth century was a flourishing time for many Mainers, but those years of Maine made superior ships, under full sail, visiting ports all over the world, would now come to a close. The packets, schooners, square riggers, and the famous clippers designed by Donald McKay, with masts so high sailors jokingly said it was an overnight journey to climb up and down, would disappear.

Still, the maritime history of Maine is very much alive today in the town of Bath, known as the cradle of American shipbuilding. The Bath Iron Works, always considered one of the best shipyards in America, continues on with pride and integrity. Modern destroyers, built here presently, have a reputation as being among the best ships in the world. Recently, General Dynamics, owner of the shipyard, was awarded contracts for a new LCS class combat ship with a trimaran hull that will enable the ship to reach speeds of up to sixty knots. The yard is also building a new highly technical Zumwalt Class destroyer. Any crew that sails on a Bath built ship knows that they have a solid ship under them, built with state of the art technology, the best materials, and the pride and superb craftsmanship of skilled Maine shipbuilders.

Modern Ship Construction at Bath Iron Works

Nostalgia

A True "Mainer"

Someone once said that "nostalgia is memory with the pain removed." When we think back to the "way life was" we remember a time that seemed simpler and less complex; when life was experienced one day at a time – "the way life should be" as the Maine motto suggests. These times will never be forgotten, but they are often remembered with an extra coat of varnish that gives them a bright glossy shine.

Many people today stereotype a true "Mainer" as one who lives a much simpler and laidback life. A true Mainer is one who was born and raised here, as was their father and mother - and at the very least, their grandparents too! They are very independent, conservative in a thrifty sense, self sufficient, outspoken and truthful. Perhaps they don't take to strangers as fast as they should, but their friendship and trust can be easily earned.

I like to think that most coastal Mainers come across as common folks – people who love baked beans, blueberry pie, and hard work. We seem to represent a nostalgic story of small saltwater farms, down east cozy homes, stone walls, fishing shacks, piers, and small industry. We are portrayed as living a life that has been molded by hardheaded realism, wisdom and common sense. We are proud of our heritage and we are proud to be self-disciplined Mainers, sharing our traditions and experiences of life which have been passed down to us from generation to generation.

One of the favorite periods of my life, which I remember with this nostalgic glow, are the years between the great depression of 1929 through the end of World War II in 1945. I have always felt that this period of time had a tremendous impact on my life and that these years had a tremendous influence on the New England culture.

The Author at Nubble Light, York Beach, Maine 1946

Our grandparents and parents who were born between the 1870's and the early 1900's were from a period of old fashioned manners. They seemed to instill their strict proper ways into our character: respect others; obey elders; do the right thing and follow regulations. These were the passwords that enabled you to travel through life. A handshake was a contract and truth wasn't a catchword.

We didn't have much professional medical care, most medicines were home remedies prepared by Mom. Herbs, sulfur bags worn around the neck, onion plasters, cod liver oil and plenty of fresh air were often prescribed. Pipe smoke from Gramp's or Dad's pipe was blown into your ears to ease the pain from earaches. Kerosene removed lice from your hair. Doctors made house calls to deliver babies, set bones and take out tonsils. Under spartan conditions they performed some extraordinary medical procedures and sometimes bartered their services for fish, lobster or vegetables.

We had two schools in a town, one elementary and one high school. Each school had two or three rooms and the teacher taught three grade levels in the same room, one class at a time. Discipline wasn't a problem because the threat of razor straps, rulers and even a rubber hose, though seldom used, kept even the worst of the students in line. Any punishment was humiliatingly dispensed in front of the class and the parents supported the teachers. Most everyone walked to school, through storms and all types of weather conditions. Wet outer garments were hung in the boiler room by a large stove with a roaring wood fire, kept stocked by an older student. The dress code was simple – blouse and skirt for women, shirts and pants for men. Some clothes were made from grain sacks and mother and sister did lots of sewing and knitting. Students caught measles, mumps, small pox, whooping cough, polio and scarlet fever. The teachers took their jobs very seriously and because they lived in the same town, they often knew every student's entire family.

Children listened and never interrupted when an adult spoke, and they called people by title - "Uncle," "Aunt," "Mr." or "Mrs." Chewing gum was forbidden. Father's word was law. Many extended families - grampa, gramma, aunts and uncles - lived under one roof. Shopping for groceries was done in a small family-run store where butter, bacon, cheese, and fresh meat were all cut on the premises. Penny candy was popular (if a youngster had a penny). Produce sellers, milkmen, garbage men, ragmen, and scissor grinders all made house calls with their horse drawn wagons. Refrigeration was a wooden icebox filled with a block of ice delivered by the iceman. The ice melted into a pan which had to be emptied periodically. Houses had soapstone sinks, pantries, black iron stoves and everyone took a bath once a week. Dogs and cats were fed household scraps from the table. Many families had their own gardens and in every parlor, Dad had his special chair.

Families could be fairly large with six to eight children per household. Kids played games that didn't cost money or need any expensive equipment to play. Fun was self-motivated with leapfrog, hopscotch, tag, sandlot baseball, basketball and football. Every town had an area where winter sledding and skating were popular. The local churches were a big factor in everyone's life. Jobs were scarce and the lesson of the 1930's was to communicate, to reach out to one another and share, and to show kindness, compassion and justice. There is much more to life than riches. People of strength and character were molded in the 30's.

The Homefront During World War II

On a cold December 7, 1941 Mainers, like every other person in the country, were in a state of shock. At about 2:00 P.M. on that afternoon we heard the news that the Japanese had bombed Pearl Harbor. Over two thousand Americans had been killed and a large number of our naval ships (a good part of the Pacific fleet) had been destroyed. The country was united as perhaps never before in history. From 1941 to 1945 we rolled up our sleeves and went to war. After four years of toil and sacrifice, victory was ours. I believe that the experience of living through the hard times of the depression was a big factor in how people adjusted to the sacrifices necessary for fighting World War II. We never had anything, and you can't miss what you never had, so we made do with what was available. In Maine, as in most of the country, neighbors prayed for the relief of others' suffering and did what they could to help each other.

Military recruiting offices overflowed as anyone of age tried to enlist. The spirit of patriotism was electrifying. Loved ones departed to serve in all branches of the service. One of my good friends, a few years older than me, tried to enlist in the Navy but they refused him because of his poor eyesight. He went across the street and joined the Air Force where he became a very successful bombardier.

Draft Boards were soon established to increase the number of soldiers and the first "Greetings" letters were sent out to all single men between the age of eighteen and twenty-five. Married men were in the second call and married men with one child soon followed. Recruits met at the village town hall. A local group presented them with buddy packs containing razors, candy bars and stationery. Then they boarded a bus bound for the train station where they were transported directly to the training camps. Fear of never seeing a loved one again caused many tearful departures.

A family with a member serving in the military placed a small white flag with blue stars in a window. A gold star appearing in a window indicated that a life had been given up for our country. The entire community mourned the loss because in our small Maine towns everyone knew everyone else. School teachers, shopkeepers, neighbors had great memories of the service person so their loss was felt by all. We were all one big family.

Staple items were in short supply and local ration boards were set up to control the distribution of meat, sugar, cheese, butter, coffee, and canned goods. They issued stamps which were required to buy these items. Gasoline, which at the time sold for fifteen cents a gallon, was rationed according to need. There were no bicycles, appliances, automobiles, stoves, irons, refrigerators, radios or washing machines available for purchase. Everything went to the war effort.

Air raid drills were held in our schools. Kids volunteered to be airplane spotters and learned the silhouette shapes of different aircraft. Some of the high school boys became auxiliary firemen. The Civil Defense Patrols were older men who kept watch over the neighborhoods making sure that all the windows were blacked out. No light of any type could be seen at night from a house. The upper halves of cars' headlights were taped over to reduce the size of the beams.

Factories and mills ran twenty-four hours a day. Busses and trains brought workers to work. Scrap drives to collect metal, paper and rubber were very common. Those not serving in the military were probably in some unpaid volunteer group contributing to the war effort. Posters, news, songs, paintings and even Christmas cards were illustrated with patriotic war themes like "Together we can win." Newspapers were smaller to conserve paper and because there was not much to sell or advertise.

Victory in Europe came on May 7, 1945 and victory over Japan was achieved later that year on September 2. To rise from the depths of the depression and mount such an enormous successful war effort required the sacrifice of the entire nation and we continue to honor these people today as America's "greatest generation."

Margaret Dixon - Rosie the Riveter, South Portland, Maine

From 1942 to 1945, the New England Shipbuilding Corporation operated two shipyards in South Portland, Maine which turned out a remarkable two hundred and sixty-six Liberty ships – armed transports that carried huge amounts of cargo (armaments and supplies) to Europe. The world's democracies were fighting for their lives and these "ugly ducklings" (as President Franklin Roosevelt called them) were a large factor in the success of the war. Significantly aided by the women's work force, the output from these shipyards has to be considered one of Maine's greatest industrial achievements. The yards ran at full speed, around the clock, and each ship was built in just fifty-two days by the thirty thousand-plus workers that included more than

Courtesy of Portland Harbor Museum, South Portland Shipyard Society Collection

The East End Shipyard

Seven Liberty ships were constructed at one time in this busy shipyard in South Portland, Maine.

thirty-five hundred women. These were the true "Rosie the Riveters" and "Wendy the Welders."

Margaret Dixon, who now lives in York Harbor, worked in a South Portland shipyard during the war. She had eleven brothers in the service and all survived. Each day she woke up at 4:30 A.M. to get ready for her 5:30 shift, for which she would earn eighty-two cents an hour. She rented a two bedroom one bath apartment for $12.00 per month and, like many others, she bought war bonds with her extra cash. The top pay for a woman was $1.20 per hour and she could work no more than fifty-four hours a week. Men could work more hours and they were paid more money.

Old York Historical Society Collection, Gift of John Bardwell

Margaret donned her leather bib overalls and leather jacket, grabbed her gloves and lunch pail and walked from her apartment to the train tracks. One of the trains that carried supplies to the shipyard picked her up, and a short time later she was inside the yard. She picked up a lug box of welding rods and some welding tongs and headed over to a flat platform where she would spend the rest of her day. She tied up her hair with a bandana and put on a helmet with safety glasses attached.

A fifteen ton crane dropped a large laminated sheet of steel onto her platform. Other women workers, called burners, had already burned holes into the plate. A second metal plate was then put in place by the crane and Margaret would weld the two together. The work was hard and required strength, skill and guts. The women were between the ages of eighteen and fifty, some with families and some without. Many of the women had husbands in the service and this gave them a furious patriotic drive and pride in what they were doing for the war effort. Quite a few women had joined the work force for the first time and most had never worked as laborers.

Margaret finished welding the plates together in about thirty minutes. The completed section was hauled away to the dry dock where it would be installed on the ship's skeleton, and two more pieces were lowered onto her platform, starting the process all over again. There were no coffee breaks, but she did get a half hour lunch break in the middle of her shift. All of the work in the yard was performed outdoors in all types of Maine weather including the severe winter cold and intense summer heat.

Working in the shipyard was dangerous as evidenced by the $5000 insurance paid if a worker died while on the job. Safety was a high priority and the yard had a force of people to oversee that every job was as safe as possible. Huge cranes swung heavy pieces of material overhead while torches burned holes through steel and welders' sparks flew everywhere in the yard. The noise level was deafening as seven ships were under construction simultaneously at all times.

When completed, the Liberty ships were each four hundred and forty-one feet long. Three large steel masts rose up from the flush decks, supporting boom cranes that loaded cargo into separate holds that lay below the five deck hatches. Over twenty-seven hundred ships were constructed in the United States, the largest number of American ships ever built from the same design. Each ship carried at least four anti-aircraft guns, two aft and two forward, and they had what is known as a "tub" which contained two additional guns. A crew of forty-five men manned these slow but dependable workhorses.

Some ships were built on "ways" and were launched when blocks holding the ship back were cut to allow it to slide down the way into the water. Others were completely built in a basin which was flooded after the ship was finished to allow it to float free. Each ship was named for a well known person and christened with a bottle of champagne. The workers took great pride in every ship that left their shipyard, but they never knew what became of them after they sailed out of the harbor. Many Liberty ships were sunk by German submarines as they convoyed back and forth across the Atlantic.

At the end of her hard eight hour shift, Margaret returned her welding tongs at about 1:30 in the afternoon. She usually took a bus back to her apartment where she cleaned the shipyard grime from her clothes to get ready for the next day.

After the war with Germany ended, some Liberty ships hauled cargo, supplies and troops to Hawaii. When the war with Japan ended, the ships became the backbone of the world's tramp steamer merchant fleet. Finally they were too slow, old, and expensive to operate. Most of the surviving ships were cut up and sunk in the Caribbean and Pacific Oceans where they became fishing reefs abundant with sea life. The only Liberty ship that exists today in its original configuration is the *Jeremiah O'Brien* which serves as a floating Liberty ship museum in San Francisco, California. This ship was launched on June 19, 1943 after a record construction time of only forty days in one of the South Portland shipyards.

At the conclusion of the war Margaret Dixon and the rest of the "Rosie the Riveters" returned to their homes or found other employment. The women's labor force that was pressed into action in 1942 changed the work force in America forever. On June 25, 1999 the United States Post Office commemorated the

"Rosies" of World War II by issuing a stamp in honor of their efforts. The great Liberty ship builders, and the women who worked from the keels to the towers with patriotism and pride, left us a great legacy. They were the end of an era that changed the world.

Margaret Dixon

Liberty Ship Monument
South Portland

German U-boats – The Threat to Our Shores

Throughout World War II German subs were a menace up and down the coast of Maine. The threat of a landing from one of these U-boats was very real, and Americans all along the eastern seaboard kept a watchful eye. In northern Maine, two spies or potential saboteurs were spotted walking along the road toward town. They had been dropped off from a U-boat as part of a spy team working in the area. The young woman who first saw them knew they weren't from the area because of the way they were dressed – Maine men walking in the middle of winter don't wear top coats and dress shoes. She notified the authorities who traced the men to Boston where they were quickly apprehended.

During the war, many Maine coast residents reported finding footprints in fresh fallen snow. The paths led up from the harbors but no footprints returned, which meant that someone had to have been dropped off by the shore. In other small coastal towns stores were broken into during the night and food was taken. The footprint paths led right back to the harbors, suggesting that subs had sent some crew members in to get supplies.

After the war, a German submarine captain told how his sub submerged in the water just off Boothbay Harbor and watched as Brown's Wharf burned to the ground. Another sub commander mentioned following large ships into Portsmouth Harbor, sailing just under the stern of a large boat. He stayed in the area for a couple of days, took pictures and then followed another large ship out of the harbor the same way.

Portland, Kittery and Portsmouth harbors were protected by large steel submarine nets that were stretched out and submerged across the channels blocking entrance into the harbors. They were heavily anchored on the shoreline and set in place every night with heavy winches, large machines and the aid of a tugboat. Some of the local fishermen who returned to the harbor after the nets were put in place for the evening had to sleep in their lobster boats in sheltered bays nearby. A few reported hearing the voices of German sailors, probably from submarines that surfaced to charge their batteries. Some of the nets were rigged with mines which would explode on impact or could be ignited by a shore battery. Thirteen mines could be planted in fifty-one minutes. The forts protecting the harbors had their own mine houses. All of the coastal batteries were well fortified.

Five major forts protected the Kittery/Portsmouth area and the major fort in Portland was Fort Williams. Guns, barracks, mess halls, hospital buildings, fire stations, plotting rooms, towers and powder rooms were spread throughout the grounds. A series of tunnels connected rooms and hallways. An officers' club, general quarters and even a theater were on the base. These forts were state of the art during WWII and fortunately no combative shots were ever fired.

Laying Mines in
Portland Harbor

War Games Inside
The Fort

Fort Levett and
Portland Harbor 1946

Firing the ten inch guns from a fort in Portland Harbor. Top picture shows the crew cleaning the gun, bottom picture shows a direct hit.

Old York Historical Society Collection, Gift of John Bardwell

German U-boat Surrenders

On May 14, 1945 the German submarine U-805 surrendered off of Portsmouth, NH. This was a Type IXC/40 boat. Note the American flag and American sailors on board the vessel.

At one time Peaks Island, just off the coast of Portland, was being armed with sixteen inch guns. A Liberty ship was used to get the guns over to the island. When the guns were in place a few days later, the coastal defense test fired them, breaking almost every window on the island! The blast even shook the stove in the kitchen at Portland Head Light, as noted by Keeper Sterling who reported watching a metal tea pot and some iron frying pans begin to dance.

Today these forts are a part of history, remnants of cement and stone. The batteries have all been sealed; many have been turned over to the state or local towns. A few have been preserved as parks. Cape Elizabeth's Fort Williams was decommissioned in 1963 and purchased by the town. The site has become one of the most beautiful public parks on the Atlantic coast, enjoyed not only by the residents, but by over a million tourists who visit here annually. It is also home to Maine's oldest, most historic and perhaps most photographed lighthouse, the beautiful Portland Head Light.

An interesting WWII U-boat encounter took place near the Nubble Lighthouse in York Beach, Maine - another example of a truly beautiful lighthouse. From 1942 to 1945 the Nubble was part of the United States military coastal fortifications. Observation towers were erected on the island and military personnel were stationed here to watch for German U-boats.

Frank Philbrick, a veteran of WWI and like many other men, too old for active service in WWII, was spending his time as commander of the Coast Guard Reserve Unit that went in and out of York Harbor. Frank was patrolling in his forty foot auxiliary Coast Guard boat when he encountered a German sub recharging its batteries. Frank was not armed so he returned to York Harbor where he notified the Coast Guard in Portsmouth and they took over. They sent out a destroyer, found the sub just south of Boon Island, Maine's tallest lighthouse eight miles out to sea, and destroyed the submarine with a depth charge attack.

Boon Island is nothing more than four acres of ledge just fourteen feet above sea level. The crew that maintained the lighthouse witnessed several encounters with German submarines. One evening, just before dusk, the watch reported a sub one half mile east of the island. The German sub surfaced and a few sailors scrambled up to its deck. They quickly inspected

71

their anti-aircraft gun, then the submarine submerged and was gone. A chase was organized but to no avail. The sub slipped away in the deep water just off the east side of Boon Island. The lighthouse crew kept watch twenty-four hours a day from a watch tower they had built on the island as well as from the lighthouse lens room, one hundred and thirty-three feet above sea level.

Old York Historical Society Collection, Gift of John Bardwell

German U-boat Crew Awaiting Confinement At Portsmouth Naval Prison

Fate of the USS Eagle PE-56 and the U-853

One of the more tragic U-boat incidents that occurred in Maine happened just outside of Portland Harbor on Monday April 23, 1945. The war against Germany was almost over. As previously mentioned, Portland was an important naval command post during the war. The USS *Eagle* PE-56, a converted WWI sub chaser just over two hundred feet long, with a top speed of just eighteen knots, was certainly not one of our modern war machines. She was nearing the end of a distinguished, well rounded naval career, having recently completed service as a search and rescue vessel. Her current assignment in Portland was to tow targets for naval aircraft bombing practice by Grumman Avengers off the coast of Cape Elizabeth.

On that fateful Monday the USS *Eagle* PE-56 went out to her target area, about nine miles southeast of Portland where over two hundred feet of water was under her hull. She had left the harbor at about 8:00 AM and just after noon the *Eagle* was shaken by a terrific explosion. The ship's stern sank in just five minutes; the bow followed, plunging into the deep icy water about twenty minutes later. Forty-nine brave men died in the explosion and only thirteen survived. Eyewitnesses had seen the conning tower of a German U-boat nearby and reported its number "U-853" to authorities. It appeared that the men were the victims of a torpedo fired by the two hundred and fifty-two foot submarine.

After a complete investigation the Navy couldn't determine if the *Eagle* had been sunk as a result of the German submarine's actions, or the victim of an unknown explosion. Because the ruling

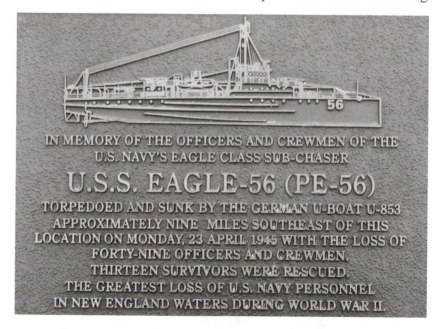

IN MEMORY OF THE OFFICERS AND CREWMEN OF THE
U.S. NAVY'S EAGLE CLASS SUB-CHASER

U.S.S. EAGLE-56 (PE-56)

TORPEDOED AND SUNK BY THE GERMAN U-BOAT U-853
APPROXIMATELY NINE MILES SOUTHEAST OF THIS
LOCATION ON MONDAY, 23 APRIL 1945 WITH THE LOSS OF
FORTY-NINE OFFICERS AND CREWMEN.
THIRTEEN SURVIVORS WERE RESCUED.
THE GREATEST LOSS OF U.S. NAVY PERSONNEL
IN NEW ENGLAND WATERS DURING WORLD WAR II.

was undetermined, it meant that the forty-nine brave men who died and the thirteen survivors would not receive the proper decorations or pensions for men wounded or killed by enemy action. After many years of lobbying and the diligent pursuit of justice, the relatives of the victims and Paul Lawton, Esquire (a Naval Historian) were able to present the true facts of the incident to the Chief of Naval Operations. The original ruling was officially changed to record the loss of the ship as a direct result of enemy action by the German submarine U-853. Fifty-six years after the sinking, the appropriate purple hearts and other decorations were justly awarded to the families and surviving crew members of the USS *Eagle* PE-56.

Soon after it attacked the *Eagle*, the U-853 was itself sunk just before midnight on May 5, 1945. At about 5:30 that evening, the submarine fired a torpedo that hit the SS Black Point, a coal ship, off Point Judith, Rhode Island. The captain of the Black Point, Charles Prior, was a Mainer. This was the last American ship sunk by the Germans in World War II, just two days before they surrendered. Captain Prior and thirty-three of his men were rescued, but twelve crewmembers died in the attack. After an

United States Coast Guard Photo

Scratch another U-boat
Crewmen paint an "authorized" U-boat silhouette aboard *Moberly* for receiving credit for the destruction of U-853.

intensive search by the Americans, the German U-boat was located six hours later. The sailors on the navy ship USS *Atherton* and the Coast Guard ship USS *Moberly* made sure that the German submarine was totally destroyed and on the bottom of the sea. There were no survivors. The sea war in the Atlantic had claimed over seven hundred merchant ships and over six thousand merchant seamen as victims of the German submarines. Many of these were Liberty ships built in Portland shipyards and merchant seamen from our Maine towns.

Commanding Officer, Ensign Henry Tilton

Back in Portland on that fatal day, Monday April 23, 1945 Ensign Henry Tilton had just left his cabin and was headed for the galley for his first cup of coffee and some breakfast. The *Eagle* had just sailed by on its way out to the training area. Henry was the commanding officer of the US Coast Guard Patrol Boat 428. His ship and crew had been assigned to the harbor, where one of their tasks was to help with the development of better electronic communications among naval destroyers. Because

Photo Courtesy of Henry Tilton

U.S. Coast Guard Patrol Boat

Portland Harbor was a staging area for many convoys of ships that crossed the Atlantic, destroyer escorts frequently sailed in and out of Portland waters. Henry's ship was docked at State Street Pier. She was eighty-three feet long and had just cruised in from Rockland, Maine where she had been engaged in patrol work.

Ensign Tilton heard the news about the USS *Eagle* in the early afternoon from Chief Boatswains Mate Calvin McNulty. As he reflected upon the events of that day, he said there was no panic in the area. The attack on the ship was not considered an immediate threat to Portland and no alerts were issued to the boats secured in the harbor. The Navy did send several attack destroyers out to the target area to conduct an anti-submarine sweeping maneuver, but the city did not respond with a general alarm of any kind. Seasoned veterans of the war and the commanders of the base didn't panic. Officers returned to their homes that evening, sailors went on liberty, and business carried on as usual.

Henry had enlisted in the Coast Guard in 1943. He was married and had one child. He went through the Reserve Officers Training School and graduated from the US Coast Guard Academy in December of 1943. A short time later he was assigned to the European theater, and along with tons of other war material, his boat was loaded onto a freighter and he headed out across the Atlantic. As an Ensign on June 6, 1944, he participated in the D-Day landing at Normandy Beach. His mission was to help rescue several hundred soldiers who were wounded in the shallow waters as they landed on the beaches in the thick of heavy enemy fire. The small patrol boats were perfectly suited for this assignment and, as we all know, these men did a remarkable job.

After the Normandy invasion his boat patrolled the English Channel, a tough and tricky area to navigate as the seas can become very rough. Their mission here was to rescue American and British servicemen whose ships had been blown up by German U-boats or one of the many German mines. These Coast Guard men performed their duty under very difficult circumstances, pulling men from burning oil soaked waters, many times under fire from the enemy sub's guns, in deep icy water while fighting heavy seas. In December of 1944 Henry arrived back in the United States and began his North Atlantic duty in New England waters.

From Portland his boat escorted freighters from Penobscot Bay to Boston. The difference between some freighters and Liberty ships was difficult to define - Henry said it was like looking at a GMC truck or an International truck, so many looked alike. When a ship left the harbor they communicated with the other vessels by signal lights, flashing codes back and forth. Radio silence kept the German U-boats from discovering their location.

Old York Historical Society Collection, Gift of John Bardwell

Just outside of Boston, two or three miles east of Graves Light, the freighters would rendezvous with anywhere from fifty to one hundred ships and sail for Europe in a convoy protected by up to ten destroyers. Loaded ships were not allowed in Boston Harbor for obvious reasons – if an ammunition ship blew up, the damage to the city would be devastating. The escort commander assigned to one of the four hundred foot destroyers was in charge of the entire convoy, which also consisted of several three hundred fifteen foot Bath built Destroyer Escorts (DE's) and English Corvettes. After Henry successfully escorted his ship to Boston, he would return to Maine where he might pick up a small fuel tanker in Searsport and escort it back to Portland. In the Maine mid-coast region the ships couldn't hug the coastline. They were in the Gulf of Maine and vulnerable to German submarine torpedoes.

Fourteen days after the attack of the USS *Eagle*, Germany surrendered. The document was signed at 2:41 AM in a little schoolhouse in the French city of Reims. The war was over. Henry Tilton remained on active duty until January of 1946 when he was relieved of his command of the sub chaser SC672 and he was placed on inactive duty.

When we think of the significant impact and contribution the Portland area had in World War II we must also think of the thousands of Maine merchant marines, civilians who served and sailed on the Liberty ships, freighters, and tankers that carried tons of supplies and cargo across the Atlantic. At the beginning of the war they suffered heavy casualties. They were sitting ducks for the German submarines that patrolled our shores. Oil slicks and debris that washed up on a beach were grim evidence of an attack. It has been estimated that as many as six thousand of these brave civilians died during the war. We built the ships necessary to protect the convoys, but the crossings were never easy or safe. Throughout the sea war in the Atlantic these brave men served their country well.

Henry Tilton, Kennebunk, Maine

A Day in the Life of a Maine Lobsterman

Jeremy Willey of Owls Head, Maine

The famous flavor of a "real Maine" lobster dinner draws thousands of visitors to our state, but many of these people have no conception of what lobsters really look like or how they are caught. Most people think the natural color of the lobster is red - an easy mistake because all but a few of the souvenir lobsters sold in the local gift shops are red. A live lobster's shell is actually a dark muddy green (although one in every ten thousand lobsters caught is blue and one in a quarter million is yellow) but when they are cooked their shells all turn bright red.

The "true" lobsters, as I call them, are found up here in the Gulf of Maine in the Atlantic Ocean from Cape Cod north to Nova Scotia. Lobsters date back to the days of the dinosaurs, surviving all these years because, believe it or not, they are aggressive as they move around the bottom of the sea. As they scavenge the ocean floor searching for food, they don't back down if challenged by other species of sea life. Although lobsters have very limited eyesight, they make up for it with a keen sense of smell. They can detect and follow scents with their antennae which let them know what they are pursuing - or what is pursuing them! They also give off a distinctive scent which other lobsters can detect.

As with most wildlife, the larger, stronger, older males dominate and are very protective of their flock of female lobsters called "hens." They aren't afraid to fight off challengers, defending themselves with their two claws aptly named the "crusher" and the "ripper." The larger crusher claw can crush up to one hundred pounds per square inch, enough pressure to split a big clam shell open with one pinch. The thinner ripper claw takes out the meat of whatever food the large claw has crushed.

Many families in Maine earn their livelihoods from the lobster industry. Boat builders, trap builders, bait suppliers, lobster dealers, restaurant owners and their employees are all dependent upon the local lobster fishermen. In 2006, over fifty million pounds of lobster were caught off the Maine shore.

Jeremy Willey, twenty-seven years old, fishes for lobster in the waters off Owls Head, Maine. He is a fifth generation lobsterman. His great-great grandfather and his great grandfather lived and fished in Owls Head and his grandfather and father live and lobster in the same area today. It doesn't get any more Maine than this! Jeremy has had his license since birth, and he started lobstering in his dad's boat when he was just seven years old, filling bait bags and doing odd jobs. At eighteen he purchased his own boat, renewed his license and was in business for himself, carrying on the tradition of his proud family. One of his greatest pleasures is meeting his grandfather and father out to sea, each in their own boats, pulling along side each other to swap a few yarns.

Lobstermen can't haul traps on Sundays from June through August and they are prohibited from fishing from the half hour after sunset to the half hour before sunrise from June through October. But every available fishing day at 4:00AM, Jeremy and Jodi Saucier, his sternwoman (and fiancé who works by his side) wake up to the weather broadcast on the local radio station. They listen to the report, and unless the winds are over twenty-five knots and/or the seas are running above ten feet, they get ready to go. They eat breakfast, pack a lunch, fill the thermos with coffee, grab a couple of snacks and several bottles of fresh water, and head off in their truck by 4:30. Once in a great while they stop at the local breakfast nook and enjoy eggs, bacon and hot muffins. They catch up on the news with a few of the other fishermen whom they usually only get to wave at when passing their boats at sea. And so begins another twelve to fourteen hour day.

They drive the two miles to Ash Point, park the truck, load their gear into a little dinghy, and Jeremy rows out to his thirty-six foot lobster boat. The boat was built in Kennebunkport by Herb Baum, a man famous for down east lobster boats, considered to be some of the most seaworthy and practical. It is a beautiful boat in both function and design. Mike Flannagen had the boat built in 1973 and he named it after his daughter, "Katherine Ellen." Since it is bad luck to change the name of a boat, Jeremy kept the name. Soon after Jeremy got the boat, his grandfather stopped by one day. "You know, Katherine Ellen is your grandmother's name," he said. Once Jeremy heard this he knew that he would never change the name.

Courtesy Jeremy Willey

Jodi and Jeremy climb aboard the boat, secure the dinghy to the mooring, and the big boat is underway. The first stop is the fishermen's co-op for fuel and bait. The co-op is a major part of the lobsterman's life. He buys all of his supplies there: diesel for the boat; oil; gloves; paper towels; and fish bait. He also sells his catch through the co-op. It is owned by a group of local fishermen, with each fisherman buying a membership that is good for life.

All the pier workers and the accountants who keep the books work for the fishermen. A board of directors elected by the fishermen oversees the activities of the co-op. Jeremy is one of sixty-five members of his co-op which also includes about ten lobstermen's kids – future fishermen!

Jeremy fuels up the boat and Jodi loads up about seven or eight bushels of bait. She dumps six trays, about a bushel and a half each, of herring into the bait box and they head out from the pier. Jeremy points the bow towards his fishing area and away they go.

Courtesy Jeremy Willey

Jeremy Willey

Many folks don't realize that lobstermen are restricted to fishing in specific areas that are regulated by the state and the federal government. Federal license laws restrict them to fishing no more than three miles out from the nearest point of land and fishing beyond the three-mile limit requires a special federal permit. Lobsters can travel about four hundred miles per year between warm and cold water. During the summer months they will be right off our rocky coast and (hopefully) the catch is great. In the winter however, they move to deeper, warmer water further out to sea so many Maine fishermen stop fishing sometime around the first of December and start again in April or May.

Winter Storage
Boat, traps and buoys are stored during the winter.

Jeremy is licensed by the state and he is restricted to fishing in one of the clearly defined zones along the Maine coast. Each one of the zones is divided into fishing berths. He and his grandfather both fish in the Ash Point berth. Jeremy's father has a federal license as well as a state license so he can fish out beyond the three-mile limit.

State licenses are difficult to obtain. An applicant must first complete an apprenticeship of one thousand hours of fishing within a two year period. Then he or she can wait up to five years for their license because new permits are restricted in each zone and determined by the number of licenses that are surrendered. In some cases, for every five fishermen giving up a license only one new license is issued, and there is a chronological waiting list for the available permits. The maximum number of traps allowed by the state per license is eight hundred. A summer resident or local school kid can apply for a special non-commercial residential license which permits them to fish a maximum of only five traps. Unlike state permits, Federal licenses can be sold by the holders for as much as $15,000.

The two fishermen have put on their rubber boots, heavy cotton gloves and are in their orange or green Grundens – special PVC coated bib pants. On hot summer days they wear the lighter white ones, and in foul weather they also wear rain coats made from the same material. While Jeremy pilots the boat, Jodi fills small bait bags with the herring. He fishes a total of six hundred and fifty traps and will haul about one hundred and fifty to two hundred traps each day, depending upon the depth of the traps, the weather, and the number of days that a trap has been sitting. Two hundred traps will be pulled up today and after each one is unloaded, a fresh bait bag made of tiny mesh will be put into the trap. Lobsters are attracted by the strong odor of the dead fish bait.

A lobster trap is from three to four feet long and two to three feet high. Today's traps are made of plastic coated metal but in the not too distant past they were made of wood, oftentimes by the fisherman himself during the winter months when he wasn't fishing.   The old traps had two equal sections - the kitchen and the parlor - which were separated by a net, or head. Most of the new metal traps have three sections: the kitchen, a mid-parlor and the parlor. The bait is tied or hung from the trap between the kitchen and the mid-parlor.

Smelling the odor from the fish, the lobsters crawl around the trap and eventually find their way toward the bait by climbing a funnel shaped net that leads into the trap. At the top of the net, the lobsters drop into the kitchen. Because they can hardly swim, they crawl around the kitchen and eventually climb up the slider net that leads into the mid-parlor. Then they may climb up another slider and drop into the parlor. Small vents are located on each side of the trap in the parlors which enable the undersized lobsters to escape. The position of the slider nets make it almost impossible for the larger lobsters to get back out because the exit hole is about one and a half feet above the base of the trap. Most traps are dropped in water about sixty feet deep, but some can go down to four hundred feet. Compartments containing cement blocks or bricks are built into the traps which keep them in place on the sea bottom.

A Modern Lobster Trap

Jeremy holds up one of his traps. The kitchen section of the trap is on the right, mid parlor and then parlor on the left. Note the escape hatches on the side of the cage in the parlor.

The basic design of the trap is the same as it was a hundred years ago. In the olden days some of the lobstermen wove their own nets and bait bags and built their own wooden buoys and traps during the winter. Some of their traps had a rounded top, as opposed to flat, because they felt that the arch or bow design gave the trap more strength and stability. Today's wire traps weigh about fifty pounds and are much more durable than wooden traps. They also contain biodegradable escape hatches – if a trap is lost these will eventually disintegrate and provide an escape route for any trapped lobsters.

Jeremy checks his navigational equipment and sets his course for the first of the yellow and red buoys that mark his traps. Many changes have taken place since the early days when a lobsterman fished from a wooden dory rowed by hand, with nothing more than a simple compass to navigate by. In those days the fishermen pulled each trap from the water by hand. They knew where their traps were by looking at landmarks, such as a church steeple or the tip of an island. Can you imagine what carrying traps, buoys and rope on the stern and bow of a two ended dory, through strong winds, rain, and heavy seas, must have been like?

Today, Jeremy uses a plotter on his boat to mark his routes. It can also be programmed to direct him to his lobster buoys. It provides the average depth of the sea, indicating any underwater ledges, and shows the distance to the nearest land. He has to know the depth of the ocean everywhere he has traps, and he must calculate the tide to provide enough rope, or warp, from the buoy to the trap. If he makes a mistake, his buoy will be floating underwater at high tide and he won't be able to retrieve it. The electronic gear alone can cost about $2500. For someone entering the lobster fishing business today they would need to invest about $100,000 and this would only purchase used equipment.

He sees the yellow top and red bottom of his first buoy. Like every other lobsterman, Jeremy has his own distinctively colored buoys which are registered with the state and his license number is burned onto the side of each one. Years ago the buoys were made from wood but these caused extensive damage to boat propellers when they were hit. Successful lobbying by other boaters resulted in legislation that now requires Styrofoam buoys which will disintegrate when hit. These buoys are much lighter and easier to handle.

Jeremy points the bow into the tide and he and Jodi get ready. He is holding the gaff stick, a six foot oak pole with a hook, in his right hand. He snatches the buoy by hooking onto the plastic ring floating on the bottom of the red side. The buoy is brought aboard and the line is put into the hauler, or winch, a round wheel suspended from the cabin that spins with the aid of the boat motor and pulls the rope up at a good fast pace. He uses extreme caution when placing the line on the hauler; one slip and his fingers, hand or arm could get caught between the rope and the spindle which could cause a severe injury.

Courtesy Jeremy Willey
Sunrise Through The Davit

This first buoy marks a pair of traps – two traps connected to each other with a line and a single buoy. Connecting the traps conserves rope and buoys and allows the fishermen to haul their gear faster. The first trap breaks the surface of the water and he hauls it onboard. He quickly slides it down to Jodi who opens it, cleans it out, and re-baits it while Jeremy hauls in the second trap and prepares it for its return trip to the sea. He steers the boat in a circle and in just a few seconds he drops his trap overboard. Jodi waits for the rope to come tight and then she pushes her trap back into the water. Once again they use extreme caution as the warp line moves quickly across the deck. If the rope tangles in their feet they can be taken overboard and carried down into the icy depths of the sea. If this were to happen, their heavy boots and gear would make it almost impossible to escape, so lobstermen carry a sharp knife in their pockets at all times, with the hopes of successfully cutting the rope. They make a point of knowing where their feet are, and where the rope is, at all times.

Sometimes two buoys can mark a string of up to ten traps. One buoy tied to each end of the string of traps enables them to be fished from either end. Called a trawl, this is a good method of fishing because it saves line and keeps the traps in the same area and depth. One buoy marking a string of traps saves time because it is easier to find than ten randomly placed buoys. A trawl can also prevent the loss of the traps if a power boat runs over a buoy or line, since many boats are equipped with a cage and mechanism near the propeller that will cut a line if it becomes entangled. This avoids expensive damage to the boat, but if the traps aren't set in a string, the fisherman bears the cost of a cut line because he loses his buoy and his trap which can cost over $85.00 to replace.

Jeremy has made a large circle with the boat as he hauled in his first two traps and sent them back. He uses as few boat movements as possible. His traps are set about a tenth of a mile apart and they only have one hundred and ninety-eight more to go! The next trap is a single. When Jeremy opens the trap he finds a couple of lobsters in the parlor. The first looks short. He places a standard metal measuring gage against the lobster's back. A legal Maine lobster has to be between 3 ¼ inches to 5 inches long from its eye to the beginning of its tail. It's a "short" and he carefully throws it back into the ocean. As a conservation measure, the state wants the lobsters to complete at least one mating season and based upon their small size, the shorts are too young and must be thrown back. Large lobsters (greater than five inches from back to eye) produce more offspring, so they are also thrown back. A chicken lobster, the most popular size served in restaurants, weighs 1 ¼ pounds and is at least seven years old. A five pound lobster would be about thirty years old.

Courtesy Jeremy Willey

Sternwoman Jodi Saucier holds up an oversized lobster, which had to be thrown back. Note the powerful claws.

The other lobster in the trap is a keeper and Jeremy puts it in a box called the banding tray. Jodi grabs the banding pliers and quickly bands the claws. A small but strong rubber band is placed around each of the claws, preventing them from opening. When lobsters are confined in close quarters they become aggressive and attack and cannibalize each other. The bands stop them from fighting. They also prevent the creatures from pinching the fisherman and causing a potentially painful injury.

An interesting promotion was used in the summer of 2006 when lobsters caught by Maine fishermen had their claws secured by yellow elastic bands printed with "This is a Maine Lobster." This distinguished the lobsters caught in Maine waters from all of the others in the marketplace. I felt this was an unusual promotion for Maine lobstermen because the lobsters that move between New Hampshire, Maine and Canada all live in the same environment, taste the same, and no one can tell them apart. The bands clearly identified which lobsters were actually caught in Maine and a tourist would know he had the real deal!

Jeremy held the lobster by its back and tail with the claws pointed up because a stressed lobster can literally "drop" a claw. Lobsters have the ability to grow back claws, antennae, and crawlers that have been lost in a fight with another lobster or sea creature, so they may intentionally drop a claw in order to escape. Sometimes the new appendage is not as large as the original, but it still works. In any event, a one clawed lobster, or cull, is not worth as much as a complete one, so Jeremy gently tosses the lobster into the holding bin on the aft deck.

When a lobsterman comes across a seeder (female lobster carrying eggs) he is required by law to cut a V-notch in its tail and send her back into the water to lay her eggs. The V indicates that this female is productive, or seeded, and if caught again she must be returned to the sea. This is another conservation law to maintain the lobster population and protect the income of future lobstermen, the sons and daughters of the present day fishermen.

There are four female lobsters for every male. The female can carry from 30,000 to 100,000 eggs for almost a year. Then she finds a sandy area in deep water and burrows in to deposit her eggs. The male lobster stays in the area to protect her. Of these thousands of eggs, only six to eight will survive. The tiny larvae that hatch from her eggs drift with the sea currents and many are swallowed up by the plankton eaters such as herring or whales. A single school of herring can number thousands of fish, so after about one month only a few surviving lobsters fall to the bottom and begin to grow.

For the next two to three years the young lobsters will try to remain hidden from predators as they slowly develop. As they grow they shed their old shells to make room for their larger bodies. Adult lobsters continue to grow and also shed their old shells. The new shells are very soft and the lobsters are extremely vulnerable to their enemies during this time. To fill the space between their smaller body and the new larger shell, they pump water into their body cavities. These "soft shell lobsters" sell for less money per pound because they contain more water and less meat than a hard shell lobster of equal size. After it sheds, a lobster will usually eat part of the old shell which supplies nutrients to its body.

Throughout the day Jeremy and Jodi haul, empty, re-bait and reset the traps. Their work gloves are a necessity as barnacles and sea coral caught in the warp can cut their hands and the fast moving rope can cause rope burns. Also, when they reach into the traps they never know what they will find. Over the years they have discovered a variety of sea life and unusual objects. Old glass bottles, trash, and a variety of plastic containers are often found. Starfish, sand dollars, old shells, sea clams, mussels, rock crabs and sand crabs are common. Large eels, flounder, cod and other species of fish are prevalent. Some of the dead fish are cut across the spine and left in the trap – free bait that attracts more lobsters. They keep some of the live fish and take them home. Cod can be wormy when trapped close to shore because of the warm water so they become bait. Occasionally they catch a wolfish, which tastes like haddock and makes a great meal. One creature they don't like to see come up with a trap is a poison jelly fish. These are handled with caution and promptly thrown back.

Once in a great while another fishing buddy will joke around and stuff an old football or a six pack in someone's trap, although it is illegal for anyone but the licensed trap owner to handle his gear. The lobster business is very territorial and occasionally a stranger may enter new waters and encroach upon another fisherman's area. Initially the new fisherman might be warned of his transgression. He may find his buoy line tied with half hitches so it floats upside down and can't be gaffed into the boat. Hopefully, the message is understood and the violator will move his gear. If not, he might find some of his lines cut and he will lose some gear. There is an honor system among the lobstermen and for the most part they respect each other's territory and play by the rules. This is their living and they have to look out for each other.

As the day draws to a close and the last trap is back in the sea, Jeremy heads back to shore and Jodi cleans the deck. The last stop of the day, before they leave the boat, is back at the co-op where their day began. Jeremy drops off his catch and the accountant logs in his total pounds, crediting him at the going price of lobster for that day. He receives a check once a week for the number of pounds of lobster he has delivered, minus the expenses for supplies. The co-op also holds out a small amount of money per pound which is set aside as a bonus for the end of the year, along with his share of any profits the co-op made from re-selling the lobster in the marketplace. The fisherman's share is determined by the number of pounds of lobster he caught that season. The annual bonuses are presented at a banquet at the end of the season, and can range from almost nothing to as much as $100,000. Their income is not guaranteed. The fishermen live from year to year dependent upon circumstances like weather, ocean temperatures, lobster behavior and equipment reliability that are, for the most part, all beyond their control. Lobsters are one of Maine's largest income producing industries. Although it can be a very difficult vocation, the number of Maine families who fish and make a living in the industry prove that it can be worthwhile.

Lobster fishing can be rewarding but it also has many dangers. The sea is a power not to be challenged because it will always win. Fishermen have a great respect for the sea but dangerous events can occur rather rapidly and this is when the good mariners show their skill. Jeremy told me about one experience he had with a sudden change in weather this past summer.

The day started out just slightly overcast and he and Jodi left the harbor at their usual time of 5:00AM with the winds at a steady three knots. The weather stayed pretty much the same all day until they had almost reached the last traps. Without warning, the sky abruptly turned a murky jet black and the winds started to blow with a deafening roar like a passing train. Jeremy and Jodi scurried around the boat to tie down any loose gear. A brilliant flash of lightning suddenly lit up the sky. The sea picked up to fifteen-foot swells and bolts of electrical current danced everywhere around the boat. No one wants to be nearly three miles out to sea in a thirty-six foot boat with these conditions!

To make matters worse, rain was pouring down in buckets and their visibility was down to zero. They huddled together in the wheelhouse and Jeremy plowed ahead with the radar, his plotter and his spotlight to guide him. He navigated by electronics only, and pushed the boat as fast as he dared. The brilliant lightning bolts crackled all around, illuminating the angry sea and forbidding sky.

As they headed to shore, about a mile from the entrance to the harbor, there was a terrible loud bump and the boat briefly hung up then jolted forward with the crest of a wave. The two seamen were stunned and they thought the worst - they had run into a ledge. The plotter didn't show any ledges in the area. Thankfully the motor kept running and Jeremy could still steer the boat. Minutes later when the shock finally wore off from the unexplained blow, another bolt of lightning lit up the sky and the two Mainers breathed a sigh of relief when they came into the harbor. They had probably run into a floating object - a log, piling or some debris - that had been kicked up by the storm.

It was late evening when they made their way slowly to the pier. All the workers had gone home. The storm was still blowing hard so they quickly transferred their lobsters into crates, or lobster cars, tied together near the pier. They had to get the live lobsters into the pens so they could survive. They found their mooring, tied up, and then Jeremy had to row the dinghy into shore. The rain was blinding and the wind was so fierce that he had to row the tiny boat sideways. The usual ten minute trip took almost an hour. Finally they made it to the truck and drove home. A day that started at four in the morning was finally over at nearly midnight.

The next morning they were back up at four and off to the co-op to unload their previous day's catch from the crates. Then they headed back to the sea to haul another two hundred traps, all the while hoping that the weather would be favorable and the sea would be bountiful on this new day in the life of a lobsterman.

Jeremy Willey and Jodi Saucier

Conclusion

Oftentimes during a busy or hectic day when I find myself caught up in today's fast paced lifestyle, I like to stop and look at the coastal scenery around me and listen to the natural sounds that fill this glorious world. Waves rippling through beach stones; the cry of a distant gull; a quiet, calming breeze rustling the pine trees overhead; these are sounds that make time stand still. The tall church steeples that point to the heavens above, and the lighthouse towers, built on solid foundations that support never failing guiding lights, are the guardians of our past.

When I watch the sunset reflected in a tidal river, gaze at a serene saltwater farm, or see lobster traps piled high next to an old shed, I realize the connection we have to those who came before us, and to those who will follow. From the lofty to the ordinary, everyone is unique and different, and the results of our efforts are visible across the panoramic landscape of life. My grandfather watched the sun rise over the ocean at Moody Beach just as my grandchildren can watch it now, and as I sit and reflect upon the stories of our past, I realize that the dreams of our forefathers were the same as ours: peace and harmony for all.

Bill Thomson

Bibliography

Clayton, Barbara and Whitley, Kathleen. "Exploring Coastal New England - Gloucester to Kennebunk." New York, NY: Dodd Mead and Co., 1979.

Humiston, Fred. "Blue Water Men and Women." Portland, ME: Blue Water Books, 1965-1966.

King, William C. "Portraits and Principles." Springfield, MA: King, Richardson & Co. Publishers, 1894.

Snow, Edward Rowe. "Sea Mysteries and Adventures." London: Alvin Redman, 1964.

Annals of the American Pulpit; or Commemorative Notices of Distinguished American Clergymen of Various Denominations, From the Early Settlement of the Country to the Close of the Year Eighteen Hundred and Fifty-Five. Sprague, William B. Volume 1. New York: Robert Carter & Brothers, 1857. pp. 243-249.
http://books.google.com/books?id=l6fYNjtWMnoC&pg=PP12&dq=samuel+moody#PPP11,M1

Atlantic Monthly, Volume XXXV. "A Memorable Murder." Celia Thaxter. Boston: H. O. Houghton and Company, 1875. pp. 602-615.
Cornell Library, Making of America
http://cdl.library.cornell.edu/cgi-bin/moa/

Faithful Narrative of the Wicked Life and Remarkable Conversion of *Patience Boston* alias *Samson*; Who was Executed at *York*, in the County of *York, July 24th* 1735. for the Murder of BENJAMIN TROT of *Falmouth* in *Casco Bay*; a Child of about Eight Years of Age, whom she Drowned in a well. With a Preface by the Reverend Messr. *Samuel & Joseph Moody*, Pastors of the Churches in said Town. Boston: Printed and Sold by S. Kneeland and T. Green in Queen Street over against the Prison, 1738
http://xroads.virginia.edu/~MA05/peltier/conversion/boston.html

German U-boat Photo Gallery
http://www.uboataces.com/history-gallery.shtml

Naval Historical Center Website
http://www.history.navy.mil/photos/sh-usn/usnsh-e/entrp5.htm

North Carolina Office of Archives and History. "Blackbeard the Pirate and the Presumed Wreck of Queen Anne's Revenge." 2007
http://www.ah.dcr.state.nc.us/sections/maritime/blackbeard/default.htm

The Salem Witchcraft Papers, Volume 1 : verbatim transcripts of the legal documents of the Salem witchcraft outbreak of 1692 / edited by Paul Boyer and Stephen Nissenbaum.
Electronic Text Center, University of Virginia Library
http://etext.virginia.edu/etcbin/toccer-new2?id=BoySal1.sgm&images=images/
modeng&data=/texts/english/modeng/oldsalem&tag=public&part=106&division=div2

U.S.Navy Website
Department of Defense, Special Release. "Navy Designates Next-Generation Zumwalt Destroyer."
http://peoships.crane.navy.mil/DDG1000/DoDrelease_NNS060407.htm

U.S. Coast Guard Website
http://www.uscg.mil/hq/g-cp/history/U853.html

About the Author

Bill Thomson lives in Kennebunk, Maine. He was born in 1929. Bill is a retired history professor and now an author and documentary filmmaker. He spends summers as a volunteer at Portland Head Light in Cape Elizabeth, Maine and at Nubble Light in York Beach, Maine.

Winters are spent writing and sharing his stories and memoirs at local Maine schools, community organizations, nursing homes, and church groups.
Bill tries to live his daily life around the Maine slogan, "the way life should be."

His grandchildren tell him he lives life "the way it was."

It was a pleasure to use the painting *"Signal of Hope"* by Bill Sachs.

Bill Sachs was born in Baltimore, Maryland and has had an interest in drawing and painting since childhood. He graduated from the Maryland Insitute of Fine Art and later became a medical artist at the University of Maryland. He served as Art Director and Planning Analyst at the Pentagon's Office of the Secretary of Defense and later became Chief and Director of the Graphic Arts and Design Division for FEMA. During his career, Bill has received many honors for his art work, among these is the distinct honor of being the only single recipient of the Pro Patria Award, which is always given to groups or companies, for "distinguished contributions to the national defense through art and design." His studio is in Hanover, Pennsylvania.